THE FIGLI

ISSUE TWO SUMMER SEASON 2024

Naked Figleaf Press

We Give A Fig

Compiled & Edited
by Jean G-Owen

The Figlet Issue Two © Naked Figleaf Press 2024
Published by *Naked Figleaf Press* Yarmouth, Isle of Wight

ISBN: 978-1-7394770-5-9

Editor Jean G-Owen
Cover design Karl Whitmore

Please visit our website at https://nakedfigleafcollective.co.uk/the-figlet/
Or email at: jean28owen@gmail.com

Contents

I'm Writing A Novel by Jamie Britton

Editorial by Jean G-Owen

Welcome to *The Figlet Issue Two Summer 2024*, the literary magazine that gives a fig about IOW writers. I received an abundance of submissions, and selecting from such a wealth of talent has been a difficult task. Forty-eight wordsmiths and illustrators have contributed to this issue, and I am thrilled, once again, by the diversity of topics and range of styles. These include poems, short stories, observational articles and political pieces. General themes touch on language, traffic, nostalgia, metamorphoses, June brides, summer holiday homes, flower shows, love – requited and otherwise – conflict, death, animals, and much more. I've also chosen twenty pieces for the featured theme, "Footprints", which you can read about on page 80.

It was a pleasure to interview IOW writer Hillard Morley about her experiences as a novelist, and to catch up with Anmarie Bowler about her literary broadsheet *Brevity*. Also included in *The Figlet* are advertisements for up-and-coming literary events on the Island: Scarecrows & Scribbles Creative Writing Workshop at Brading Roman Villa; Isle of Wight Writers Day at Carisbrooke Priory; YARNIVAL West Wight Word Fest; and "Hear Me Now", a six-month creative writing project for LGBTQ+ people and allies.

I'd like to thank Paul Armfield for hosting the launch of *The Figlet* at Medina Bookshop, Cowes, in line with the inaugural IOW Biosphere Festival. A special thank you to Karl Whitmore for creating yet another brilliant front cover and for his other illustrations in the magazine. Thanks also to Ross Glanfield – his assistance and support are as cherished as morning coffee.

If you have any suggestions for future issues of *The Figlet*, please get in touch. And keep sending in those submissions – you'll find details of Issue Three at the back of the magazine.

Happy reading,

Jean G-Owen

Scarecrows and Scribbles
Creative Writing Workshop
Brading Roman Villa

'I had brains, and a heart also; so, having tried them both,
I should much rather have a heart.'
L. Frank Baum

Saturday 24 August
2 – 4pm
Brading Roman Villa
Morton Old Rd, Brading, Sandown PO36 0PH

Price: £12.00

Local writers Jean G-Owen and Maggie Sawkins invite you to a creative writing workshop exploring themes inspired by the popular Brading Scarecrow Festival.

Suitable for beginner and more experienced writers.

Just bring along your brain, but most importantly your heart (plus pens, pencils, notepads, paper).

Why not stroll around the Brading Scarecrow Festival before joining Jean & Maggie for nibbles at the Roman Villa café at 1pm.

Booking via Eventbrite at:
https://www.eventbrite.co.uk/e/scarecrows-scribbles-creative-writing-workshop-tickets-927870033247?aff=oddtdtcreator

3

Preface Manifesto 401, 402 & 424 by Steve Rushton

401.
I must confess a prejudice.
I'm bored by all the anecdotes
that start with lines like "I did this"
and "I did that" – I'm not the perfect
    dinner-party guest I know.
And recent stand-up comedy
along these lines I cannot stand.
And quick fire sit-com repartee –
like *Friends* and all those "housey-housey"
    shows – I hate. But give me *Scandi-*
Noir or something with a decomposing body, someone chasing
    someone else – hilarious.

402.
"So where's the decomposing body?"
    "Over there, surrounded by
a coterie of acolytes."
"Describe them." "Well, a lack of style
is prevalent, a fashionista's
    seminar it's not, although
there are some actors practising,
but mostly people shuffle papers."
    "Age?" "It ranges from the teenage
    prodigy to those without
a proper hobby." "Suspects?" "Well,
it's all of them, though they will argue
    they've been keeping decomposing
    bodies live for quite a while."
"Do you agree?" "Well, possibly."

424.

A single voice, the perfect I,
all sensitive, intuitive,
a solitary commentator
    on our lives – Romanticism
was and is, in spite of many
movements since, we still have this,
the single voice, the perfect I.

I wandered lonely as a cloud,
How do I love thee? Let me count the ways.
i like my body when it is with your
I hold with those who favor fire.
I thought that love would last forever: I was wrong.
I hope to see my Pilot face to face
When I have fears that I may cease to be
Because I could not stop for Death
As I grew older
    I lie on my back at midnight
    Now as I was young and easy
    I know Why The Caged Birds Sing
I am in need of music
    Traveling though the dark I found a deer
I saw the best minds of my generation
    I am silver and exact. I have no preconceptions.
Yes you have.

I witnessed Steve Rushton's poetry and sound project 'Ovid with Reverb' featuring
Lorrain Baggaley performed for the first time at Dimbola, Freshwater Bay in 2023,
and became an avid fan. This year, Steve published an online Google book,
Interpretations from the Dryden Translation of Ovid's Metamorphoses, which he's performed
at various venues on IOW and the mainland over the summer (see link below). The
poems included here are from his book *Preface Metamorphoses* (erbacce-press 2022),
taken from the section titled '401-430 Preface Manifesto (for wit/debate in poetry
with reference to *Scandi-Noir*)'. They offer a taste of Steve's innovative poetic talent.
    https://www.google.co.uk/books/edition/INTERPRETATIONS_FROM_T
HE_DRYDEN_TRANSLAT/zELzEAAAQBAJ?hl=en&gbpv=1

The Artist And Her Critic by Jean G-Owen

The Artist collects hair, shells and other inedibles.
Bruised fruit, errant feathers, still life,
a *cut* on her cheek from an Italian lover.
She likens trauma to a web of spiders.

Grass is greener on the underside of canvas,
she tells the Critic who thinks
he own the rights to her galleries.

He hovers on the edge of her paintings,
frames her (work) in his terms,
scrawls purple prose over her walls,
skulks off to compose her downfall.

His Promethean liver
should be eaten each day by eagles
because he knows life can't be stilled
or distilled by those who seek refuge in paint.

The Critic knows it's not right
to equate the bird in the Artist's heart
with her love of charcoal.

The Artist starts another piece,
determined to ignore He-Who-Speaks
from his *know-it-all* place –
that dark, drab, and dreary bung hole.

Q.E.D. by Emily Gillatt-Ball

When, sixteen hundred years ago, the Romans left our shores
I'm told they left a gift each public schoolboy now abhors.
I've searched for it ad nauseam, but all I found were loads
of bona fide spearheads and a lot of blooming roads.
They left those, ipso facto, every way they chose to go.
But with feet on terra firma, I preferred a quid pro quo.

So, carpe diem, we just flogged the stuff they left behind
including – caveat emptor – some flasks of dodgy wine.
In vino veritas, although I'd rather have some gin
I feel my rigor mortis is already setting in.
I shared things out pro rata with a quorum of the guys,
and if caught in flagrante, we'd prepared good alibis.

No time for a post-mortem, just accept the status quo.
I'll soon become persona non grata, time to go.
Aurora borealis must fade by light of day,
as so pass all our glories; sic transit, as they say.
Each magnum opus I create will add to my CV.
That may be a non sequitur; it's difficult, you see.

I still can't find the gift the Romans left us when they went,
unless you mean the aqueduct, I don't know what you meant.
I've asked, ad infinitum, on the Southern Vectis bus
what have the flipping Romans ever given us?

In Praise Of Public Transport by Olha Bereza

Recently, I saw a discussion on social media about public transport. Some said they wouldn't use it because they don't like being surrounded by strangers. Someone cited a quotation by Thomas Heatherwick (founder of Heatherwick Studio): "In cities that are not working well, it's the wealthy people who don't use public transport".

My time on the Isle of Wight using the amazingly well-run buses makes me an advocate for public transport. Perhaps there should even be a general disclaimer saying this conveyance is for everyone, not just the poor, the rich, or the trendy.

It is fantastic to be on the second floor of a double-decker bus – electric or hybrid – watching the beautiful views of the island on the way. There are quite a few buses on major routes, so they are never too busy, and most of the time, my favourite front-view seat is empty.

I enjoy watching the sunrise on my early morning trips. Would I prefer instead to be stuck in traffic in a small, smelly city, thinking about petrol costs and parking spaces? Maybe not (smiling).

Let's consider that one bus takes about seventy cars off the road. That is seventy tons of metal, glass, plastic and fossil fuel removed from the environment.

Something to think about, isn't it?

Old London Town by Ricky Lock

The Thames snakes around the city,
through industrial waste,
remembers its history, its blood and gore,
how Jack the Ripper stalks women to deface.

The smoke diffuses to blacken stone.
Poverty stares out for all to see,
small, grubby hands beg and plead –
a gentleman's coin would set them free.

Horse-drawn omnibus painted red
carries hordes across the Big Smoke,
pickpockets wait for a chance to strike,
leaving their victims angry and broke.

The railway comes to such relief,
steam and speed the order of the day,
trains packed with smoke and chatter:
This is the way to travel, passengers say.

Victorian London rules the world,
the largest port, international trade,
sewerage systems lead the way,
but let's not forget those Workhouses,
where children were betrayed.

#52 Bus To Westminster – A Haibun by Tim Cooper

I'm sat on the bus on the way to work, trying to write a haiku. It's so hard. The rules are so simple. You have 5 syllables, and then 7, then 5 again, a reference to a season and a parting. But if that was all you needed, then this would be a haiku: First comes the set-up/Next comes a separation/Oh, and it was Spring.

And it clearly isn't. It's crap. It lacks completely that connection between the reader and the poet, which is the bare minimum required of any art. Maybe it's because I'm counting syllables, whereas in Japanese I should be counting "On". But that's no good to me – I don't speak Japanese and I don't really know what an "On" is. And besides, there are plenty of good haiku in English which do the syllable thing, so I should be able to make it work. My phone vibrates. It's you.

"Going f drink w Freya after work. Make me something nice for when I get in? xx"

I was going to meet Dave for a game of squash. "Can't we get a takeaway?" I reply.

"Oh. Sad Face emoji. Show me you love me. Heart emoji. Do me that beef steak vindaloo you do? Big-eyed Smiley Face emoji. Pleeease? It's sooooo gooooood. Xxx"

It takes hours. No chance of meeting Dave if I agree. But if she's asking for steak, she's probably about to get her period, and if that's the case I don't want to risk annoying her. I can see Dave tomorrow, maybe. If it is her period, she's definitely going to want me out of the house.

"OK," I reply.

She sends: "Heart emoji. You're the best. Smiley emoji. Kiss emoji. Pussy cat emoji. Aubergine emoji. Water emoji".

That would be nice, I think, but there won't be any of that if she comes on tonight. I type an "8" followed by five equals signs and a greater than sign. I delete one of the equals signs – better to under-promise and over-deliver than the other way round – and hit send. I look back to my notebook and write:

I woke this morning.
Blackbirds sang, you were not there.
Oh! And it was Spring!

MEDINA
BOOKSHOP

A brilliantly bespoke selection of the best new fiction and non-fiction as well as a comprehensive range of new and second-hand local, and antiquarian maritime titles.

We also have puzzles, games, cards and stationery and an ever-changing exhibition of artworks for sale.

Medina Bookshop also has an exciting programme of musical and literary evening events, see online for details.

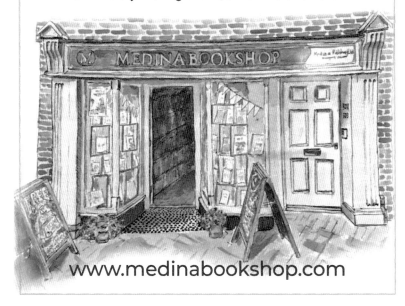

www.medinabookshop.com

The Show Must Go On by David Goodday

You're right, it is a strange way to travel. But with fares on the rise and the looks I get when travelling on public transport, I think it's a great way to save money and avoid any embarrassing situations. The one advantage of being so short is that I can fit inside my partner's case – it accompanies us to every performance. Yes, it can be a bit of a squeeze, what with all the costumes and props, but if I cross my arms and legs, it's really quite cosy.

Last night, at the King's Theatre in Southsea our show brought the house down. Tonight we're playing the Bradford Playhouse. To avoid any delays we're catching the early train.

Geoffrey, the other half of our comedy act, was behaving rather strangely last night. He didn't seem his usual flamboyant self. Maybe he's thinking of retiring or perhaps he's foolish enough to think he needs a new partner.

I know that he gets fed up with all the travelling. Being the wrong side of seventy means that he doesn't have the energy he'd had in his youth. I think the stress and strains of continually being on tour are having an impact on his health.

Fortunately, I don't have any such concerns. I'm still in relatively good nick for my age. Okay, so every now and then my joints get a bit stiff, but that's to be expected. My face still shows no signs of ageing – indeed, I don't look any older now than I did when Geoffrey and I first started in show business together.

Perhaps he's going to tell me tonight after the Bradford show. It's the kind of thing he would do. He's always been a difficult man to work with. He pulls a few strings here and there, but he's never been a comedian. I'm the one who gets him most of the laughs.

We argue a lot, sometimes over the silliest of things, and he refuses to talk to me for days when he's in one of his moods. When he finally comes around, we end up having yet another argument. All because he insists on putting words into my mouth – words I never intended to say.

It can be quite frustrating sometimes. But if I'm right and he does intend ending it all tonight, then I promise you now, I'll never speak to him again, not for as long as I live.

We've had a very long and successful career together but if he makes the break tonight then I'll have no choice but to find another partner. How else can an out-of-work ventriloquist's dummy like me earn an honest living?

The Bride by Meryl Clark

Georgia studied her reflection. There was no doubt about it; she looked great – James would call it stunning. She twisted left and right, letting the folds of her dress fan out gracefully, showing off her slender body and the exquisite pearl and crystal embroidery around the hem.

Yes, she thought. *It's just right – elegant but not overdone. Anything more would start to border on vulgar.*

Her gaze moved upwards to rest on her bosom, creamy, discreet and encased in dainty guipure lace – just enough to enchant but not shock the bishop. The ceremony was to be held in Ely Cathedral, after all.

Her face was delicate, and her large, greenish eyes positively glowed. *Hmm, I need some blusher.* She wanted to look pale and interested, not ill.

The head-dress was a circlet of wax orange blossom. It had been her mother's, beautifully preserved in black tissue from her 1940s wedding dress. Mother had borrowed her sister's wedding gown, as rationing wouldn't have allowed fabric for a new dress. The veil – her grandmother's – was of gossamer light, silk net. It just reached the hem of her gown. She could salvage enough for that; the rest was so frail that, however careful she was, her fingers made holes in the disintegrating fabric.

Now we'll see what you have to say, lady, she thought viciously. *Silly bitch. Not good enough for your James, eh? Too common?*

Her future mother-in-law had managed to dislodge two earlier fiancées. One simply had enough of the constant carping and complaints and bolted with a sales rep from Hull. The other, who got along better with the dreadful woman, had become quite ill. A mystery stomach complaint. James was very aware that as scion of the DeVeres, he was expected to marry someone capable of continuing the illustrious family line. So, with regret, he'd let her fade away to her home in County Kildare.

Perhaps the Irish brogue determined her fate in the eyes of James' mother, Georgia mused.

She shrugged. No one would ever fit her bill. Preening in the glass, she knew that she looked the part. There could be no complaints.

She heard voices in the corridor and, to her surprise, the dreaded mother-in-law swept in, accompanied by a pretty brunette. They were chatting away, heading for the wardrobe in the corner of the room.

Georgia surveyed the girl's backside as she reached into the cupboard. The first thought that came into her mind was: *Blimey! She certainly has child-bearing hips.*

The girl turned, and Georgia noticed a floor-length white frock in her arms. The girl held it up to admire herself in the mirror, passing straight through Georgia as she did so.

Georgia's second thought was: *How did that happen?*

The third was: *Maybe I shouldn't have accepted that glass of champagne from James' mother. It did taste rather odd.*

Summer Concert by Marion Carmichael

A breeze stalks around the old house,
lifts the corners of tablecloths and rugs.
Swifts dart across the violet sky,
rooks caw homeward.
Stilettos and Doc Martins crunch the gravel,
corks pop and cans hiss.
The air cools,
ghostly flowers release their scents
to mingle with smoked salmon,
sweet basil and strawberries.
The house stands aloof,
doors closed; windows shuttered
against the determined revellers
their cool boxes, ice buckets,
tables and lanterns.
A baton is raised:
some conversations stop.
In his grave an old aristo turns.

A No-Bell Prize by Jamie Britton

A Splash Of Colour by Cheryl May

One of the inmates told "Call Me Muriel" that I was stealing bananas. Muriel's the manager. She doesn't like me referring to us as inmates, but I tell it like it is. I asked how we are supposed to treat the place like our own home when there are rules and regulations. Apparently, *Thou shalt not help thyself to bananas* is one of them. I'm not good with rules.

Our lives are devoid of colour. Everything in this place is beige or magnolia, apart from the bright yellow bananas. A few vases of daffs or roses about the place wouldn't go amiss.

These windows don't let much light in. The nets could do with a drop of bleach. It's grey outside today, quite a contrast from yesterday – blue skies for our summer fête. Any excuse for a raffle and "guess the weight of the soggy fruit cake" competition. We'd have better odds guessing how many currants were in it. I know we're old, but why does the local ukulele group entertain us every time – and always including songs from the First World War in the repertoire. That was a lifetime ago, none of us remember it. Most of those ukulele players are older than us lot. I want a bit of eye candy at my time of life. A "Tom Jones" tribute act would go down a storm. I'm not sure about any of us flinging our unmentionables at him, though.

Someone suggested we get a local pop group called Wet Leg to entertain us. It's an unfortunate name for a band, especially in a place like this. Wet leg is an everyday occurrence when you get to our age. We had a lovely duo last Christmas. They were called "Koffee and Kreame", spelt with Ks instead of Cs. That's about as avant-garde as they got. They played modern tunes from the Fifties and Sixties that we all knew. The last time Kreame sang for us, she wore a lovely bright yellow off-the-shoulder chiffon dress. Admittedly, the colour clashed with her ginger hair something chronic, but it was a gorgeous dress. The sort you'd wear to a swanky film premiere. It added a much-needed splash of colour to the place.

"Call Me Muriel" installed a suggestion box in the lounge last week. It was full within the hour. Cook is still here, though. Much good the suggestion box did. I don't know if it's a combination of cheap food or cook's habit of boiling the colour and goodness out of everything, but Deliveroo is on speed dial. We haven't got the teeth to chew on a piece of rubbery meat, so why give it to us? I'd thought about going vegetarian but couldn't stomach the prospect of cabbage, pulses and flatulence for the rest of my days.

So, what if I'm taking bananas? It's my act of rebellion.

Cheryl May enjoys writing plays and comedy sketches. She has over a hundred published scripts under her pen name Cheryl Barrett. Her debut poetry collection *Not Just Desserts* was published by Naked Figleaf Press in April 2024. Cheryl enjoys performing and brings her own brand of Mayhem to Figgy Gig events. She continues to write for *Sardines Magazine* for Amateur Theatre.

www.cherylbarrettwriter.co.uk

Chelsea Flower Show by Darren Everest

The Royal Horticultural Society's flagship event of the year is the Chelsea Flower Show. To some, winning gold at this incredible show is the pinnacle of a horticultural career. Most garden designers and plant growers dream of exhibiting here. But things are only sometimes all as they seem.

The Grand Pavilion, the show's centrepiece, is where nursery connoisseurs put up incredible displays of specialist plants and flowers: delphiniums, fuchsias, pelargoniums, chrysanthemums, clematis, roses, heucheras, Alpines, and much more fill this impressive structure. Even, with a bit of luck, one of my specialisms, sweet peas.

Outside the Pavilion, show gardens line the avenues. This is where the big money talks. Sponsored by multinational companies, the garden designers spend thousands on their vision. But, like any art form, garden design is subjective: what is lovely to one person is bloody awful to another.

Some, in the main, use plants in their designs, while others are more contemporary, with minimalist planting surrounded by hard landscaping and unusual structures. The gardens often follow the fashion of the day or try to influence the fashion of the future. Some are successful, some not so.

It's all a charade, an illusion for the masses. Almost every plant and flower has been forced out early or held back by nurseries across the UK and beyond to be ready in late May each year. Garden designs have plants in full bloom next to one another that typically flower at different times of the year. Displays in the Pavilion are all from plants that would usually be out at other times of the year.

The majority of visitors are utterly oblivious to this facade. Many are from overseas and come to Chelsea especially to see the show, unaware of when the plants would typically flower here. Many come for the status as part of their social calendar – a must for those classes who love pretty flowers and champagne!

It's clear to see all around that money talks here. Sales pitches outside are filled with glasshouses and price tags to make your eyes water. "Outdoor living", as it is called, from air-conditioned domed pods, table and chair combinations to suit every occasion, barbeques that cost more than a new kitchen and statues of wild animals, and – let's be honest – who wouldn't want a life sized gorilla or giraffe in their garden?

As a first-time visitor, it's a fantastic place to visit. Yes, it's overcrowded; if you don't get there early enough, you'll struggle to see anything before being caught up in the constant ebb and flow of crowds. However, the changes are apparent to those who have been there for many years. Specialist displays have dropped steadily, enough so that the space is now filled with "educational" displays promoting sustainable gardening and floral art competitions. Many previous exhibitors have either retired or been priced out due to the considerable costs and logistics of getting here.

The costs are phenomenal, especially for small specialist growers such as myself. Firstly, parking costs anywhere between £45-£80 per day – yes, per day. Accommodation is around £200 per night just for a bed, and you'll be there for one week. You have to stay with your stand from morning until night so there's little opportunity to eat properly. Of course, travelling through busy London traffic and the ULEZ charge add to the price.

Negotiating the sheer volume of people and vehicles on-site during the build days, all trying to unload as near their stands as possible, is a very stressful experience.

Yet none of this means the Chelsea Flower Show isn't a superb spectacle. Yes, it has changed over the years, but then what doesn't? The visitors make it all a fantastic experience, and while the logistics of taking part are immense, I am thrilled to have exhibited here.

A Green Solution by Sandy Kealty

Come ladybirds and eat my aphids!
Their rapid infestation is beyond me now.
I have rejected death by noxious spray,
stopped murdering by stealth,
but my, it's so laborious when you do it all yourself.

One by one, I pick them off
(I am retired now, so have the time),
then squash them, but the odious slime
that this produces is no use to bird or beast.
And don't you reckon, at the very least,
the outcome should increase the richness of the earth.

Even a greenfly has its worth.

Come ladybirds, and make it quick,
your intervention is required.
I've read that you eschew a garden where bugs are few.
No meagre pickings here; please, rest assured –
a scented bed, a groaning board.

Come ladybirds, deprive the farming ants.
Perhaps they, too, will fade and dwindle.
A chance, indeed, to see off yet another pest
the natural way, for Nature's way's the best.

Then, we'll engage some nematodes to slaughter all the rest.

Cloisters by Marion Carmichael

Cool shade
quiet space
well of pure water

Paved walk
clacking beads
scented white roses

Narrow way
blinding light
boundaries of box

Gothic arches
dark corners
pink stone walls

Locked gates
ordered lives
square of sky

The Holiday Home by Chris Barnes

You'll be bulldozed soon. Too old-fashioned for seaside Cornwall now. Your lovely wooden doors with Bakelite handles are thrown on a skip, along with the serpentine stone fireplace and the retro vintage flap. The pale chenille green kitchen cupboard held literally everything, especially my affection. Each glass, enamel dish, or porcelain teacup had a tale to tell – every piece as individual as the house and the elderly couple who once owned them.

I loved picking wild roses from the overgrown garden and arranging them in the old paisley vase, whose pattern perfectly matched the colours of the roses. The battered fruit from our cool box looked so much better in the old lemon fruit bowl atop the green vinyl kitchen tablecloth.

Once I had both in place, I felt we had arrived again, taking ownership of this familiar coastal hideaway. When the beds were made, the boots, shoes, and coats in the rack by the entrance, and the windows and doors flung open to let in the sea air; I would relax, letting out a long sigh of relief with anticipation of our holiday time ahead.

Then, after a reviving cup of tea, I would climb into shorts and flip flops and head straight for the beach below, leaving the house wholly unlocked in abandoned certainty of safety.

It didn't take long for the sand to enter the house. The conservatory filled with drying towels, wetsuits, swimming costumes, fishing nets, books, papers, and other paraphernalia. That's when we knew the holiday was really underway.

In the sitting room next to the serpentine fireplace was an old oak bookcase. It contained a well-thumbed, eclectic collection of ordnance survey maps, local and geological reference books and many nature and wildlife guides. My favourite was the first edition of John Betjeman's *Summoned by Bells*. I would place this in the conservatory alongside other favourites. Every holiday, I read it out loud to any family member, desperate to share my love for this author and place.

God, I hope it was saved from the house before it was demolished and all possessions hurled into the skip.

Your location, of course, was your inevitable downfall. As the Estate Agents' blurb said:

Prime coastal location ripe for development; a vast plot with room for expansion.

We'd seen it happen year after year all around the village. First, the Post Office went, and with it the village shop that had been at the heart of this ancient coastal settlement.

But we loved you as you were. You remained our connection to Kernow, our spiritual home, which we had reluctantly left many years before to settle back on the Isle of Wight to be closer to our Island family. You were just *too far away*.

So, no more walking to Harlyn, swimming in Tinker Bunny's tidal sea pool or hearing gulls crying above the slate-hung wall at Rocky Beach as the sun sets towards Trevose Head.

Sadly, you, too, have been summoned by the bells.

Heritage Vinyl by Anmarie Bowler

Kate corners her in the entry hall of the coastal holiday let that Kate's family has owned for years. Eli, who cleans the coastal holiday let, taps her phone, eyes the time and re-jigs the dense bag of laundry she's desperate to dump in her car boot.

"I've got a great little job for your daughter," Kate answers as if Eli's asked.

"She's pretty busy," Eli said.

Weed a garden, wash a car, walk a dog – odd jobs Taylor just finds odd.

"It won't take two hours, and there's £20 in it for her," Kate says.

Then, after placing cash on the hall table, Kate begins reading aloud from a coloured flyer that seems to praise timber frame sash windows while maligning their modern vinyl counterparts. Did she call replacement window installers "criminals" who commit "architectural malpractice?" A careless mix of metaphors, Eli thinks. Eli's father installed hundreds of uPVC windows from one end of the island to the other. He fell off a ladder and died while installing a uPVC window. She's always thought he jumped. Or did he fail to save himself?

"...save island homes for the sake of our island heritage. Vinyl windows are a slap in our ancestor's face. Heritage windows mean –"

Kate's emphatic patter fills the entryway where they stand and squeezes Eli, rushing excess reflection to her head. A descendant of the replacement window, Eli knows she's current, capable, and efficient. Ugly but useful, cheap and un-cheerful, she stares at Kate reading and gesticulating, finds Kate comical, and the levity quickly releases Eli from introspection's trespass.

"If I told you there aren't more than three timber sash window makers on the island, would you be surprised?" Kate asks. "The thing is, we need to funnel our young people into worthy, traditional trades. Offer them opportunities to work with their hands, be trained properly and traditionally, and make an honest living. For their sake, frankly."

Eli's certain Kate's sons won't be funnelled –

"Here's 50, no 75 flyers, for your Taylor to pop through doors next week. I'll pay in advance because, of course, I trust her."

"She's just really busy. She fell behind in maths, so she's doing extra lessons. Thanks anyway." But Taylor's a maths champ – like her granddad – the builder, the gambler, the replacement window installer

26

Kate's obviously disappointed. Kate, who pays *KO Kleaners* to employ Eli to clean Kate's second home, is definitely disappointed.

"I'll do it."

"You?"

"Absolutely. Pleasure. No problem," Eli says, offering a thin smile as she pockets the £20.

"Brilliant," Kate sings, backing out the door. "Thank you. So much. You," she points, "you're preserving your heritage." She slips inside a black SUV and drives away.

On her way home, Eli slips flyers through the mail slots of a dozen Georgian houses near her flat overlooking a car park before tossing the rest into the recycling bins behind the supermarket.

Anmarie Bowler was raised in a small town in Ohio. She is a playwright and her theatre piece *AKA* was adapted into a short film by UK director Dave Maybrick. It earned several awards on its worldwide tour of short film festivals. In 2019, Anmarie served as Head Copywriter for *The Wight Book*, a large-format book about the Island. Consistent with her obsession with *small stories*, she teamed with local photographer Zoe Barker to create Re:Box, the Island's tiniest art gallery, tucked inside a decommissioned K6 grade-listed telephone box in Ryde.

Heritage Vinyl is taken from Keeper, Anmarie's collection of flash fiction.

Focus on BREVITY and HEAR ME NOW

When Anmarie moved to IOW from London seven years ago, she wrote a short story and looked for a local literary publication where she might submit the story, only to find out the Island didn't have such a magazine.

Anmarie explains: "A full-scale glossy magazine was more than I could manage. But a handbill – an elegantly folded piece of A3 paper featuring compelling stories from Islanders for Islanders was perfectly sized in shape and ambition."

And so *Brevity* was born. This innovative literary handbill launched in October 2019. It is published bi-monthly, six times a year and is available free of charge at all Island libraries, as well as Chocolate Apothecary, Aspire Ryde, Medina Books in Cowes, The Goose Bookshop in St Helen's, Babushka Books in Shanklin, Quarr Abbey Bookshop, Ventnor Exchange, The Star Coffee & Ale House, Monkton Arts, The Freshwater Coffee House, and Coffee Nut in Ryde, to name just a few.

Anmarie comments: "Short-form expressions of all kinds really speak to me, and I'm no doubt obsessed with what is today called flash fiction. Now, along with Brevity, Island writers have another outlet for their work, The Figlet, founded by Jean G-Owen. What a wonderful publication – once you see it, you want to crack it open and start reading. Our local literary scene is growing, becoming better connected and supportive."

Hear Me Now: Workshops, Walks, and Talks

In partnership with StoneCrabs Theatre, Anmarie was awarded an Arts Council project grant for _Brevity_ to produce "Hear Me Now", a six-month creative writing project for LGBTQ+ people and allies.

The first writing workshop, held at Ryde Library, was hosted by Anmarie and award-winning short story writer, novelist, and lecturer Emily Bullock on 30 April.

George Budden, a London-based LGBTQ+ photographer who recently completed a creative residency at Dimbola House, led an inspirational walk/talk titled _Queer in Nature_ on the West Wight on 25 May. Participants met at The Red Lion in Freshwater.

Author of the queer Age of Sail _Leeward_ and _The Devil to Pay_ Katie Daysh led a "Writing Historical Fiction" workshop at One Holyrood, Newport on 8 June.

On 13 July, Island creatives Tracy Mikich and Teresa Grimaldi will lead a hands-on print workshop at Boojum & Snark in Sandown. Participants will design and print a one-off _Hear Me Now_ broadsheet featuring short-form work they've written for the project. The unique publication will be available during Pride, 19-21 July 2024.

On Sunday, July 21, Niall Moorjani, a non-binary, neurodiverse Scottish-Indian writer and storyteller, will lead a _Hear Me Now_ workshop/talk at Ryde Library and perform at the Ventnor Fringe Festival.

There are plans for a walk/talk at The National Trust's Mottistone Manor and Gardens, where participants will be inspired by the lives of mid-20th century architects and partners Paul Paget and John Seely, who worked together to restore Mottistone Manor.

The _Hear Me Now_ project will wrap up with StoneCrabs Theatre co-producing a public performance of selected short stories and audio recordings that will be featured on _Brevity's_ website.

If you would like to learn more about the Hear Me Now project, email: Caroline Diamond at caroline@stonecrabs.co.uk

or register for the free workshops/walks/talks via the _Brevity_ website: **https://brevityisland.home.blog/contact/**.

A full report of these events will appear in _The Figlet_ Issue Three, 2025.

No Means No, Doesn't It? by Jean G-Owen

It is a cliché, a well-worn fact, that sometimes opposites attract.
Boy meets girl, girl meets boy, love all round for the hoi polloi.
It should be simple. It should bring joy.

But if, when they are on a date, one mishears the other mate,
one says NO, one hears YES, that NO means willing, acquiesce.
The love story ends in a sorry mess.

How can such a simple word, be mistaken, be misheard,
which of us could ever guess, that NO could be construed as YES.
It should be law, to friend and foe, that NO on all fronts equals NO.

My efforts to advance this point, will put some noses out of joint,
I speak a language plain and clear, in case they get the wrong idea.
NO is never YES, my dear.

Mishearing leads to sordid crime. Excuses are a waste of time.
To get the wrong end of the stick, should put the culprit in the nick!
This really isn't rocket science. Mishearing is just pure defiance.

But if mishearing wins the day, what is the victim supposed to say?
Did I consent? Is it so? NO does mean YES, and YES means NO.
How much deeper does this go?

For all those folk who fail to hear, I'll say it once more
LOUD and CLEAR
so that they get the right idea: NO is never YES, my dear.
It should be law, the status quo, on all fronts equal, NO means NO.

A Bigger Boy Did It And Ran Away by Cat James

I'm reading a novel called *Woman on the Edge of Time* by Marge Piercy. Its protagonist, Connie, is captive in an asylum; locked up due to grinding poverty and circumstance. She is defeated; hair matted; experimented on. But she has a special power. Connie can travel through time and, in a particularly bleak moment on the ward, finds herself transported to a utopian future.

In it, society is collaborative. The genders are blurred; there are no specific sex-based roles. Instead of *he* or *she* people are referred to as *per* (short for *person*). Decisions are made communally. Just enough food (mostly plant-based) is provided through local farming. People only work when they have to; machines do the heavy lifting. Everyday utensils are made to last or designed to be "circular", to preserve the earth's resources.

This book, written in 1976, has been described as a feminist classic. I don't know how the story ends, but I'm hoping this alternative future becomes a reality and that if Connie gets released, she does not return to her tenement in a miserable and polluted New York, and her niece's violent pimp.

Marge's novel does not have to be fantasy. We *can* have nice things. But, for some reason, a section of humanity seems hellbent on inflicting its bullish methodology on us all. You know who I'm talking about, right?

For example, we often hear the cry: "Why aren't there more women in politics?". I know that, personally, I would not want such an adversarial and toxic workplace; where my day job is to bellow and point-score, where I might be mocked and subjugated. If a decision is to be made, I'd like to debate it civilly, with people from all walks.

I wonder if all the things which I detest about the human race: self-serving politicians, racism, hatred of the other, lack of compassion for the disadvantaged – in fact, an active desire to disadvantage others, might be due to testosterone?

I can't imagine what it's like being of the sex where one's perceived strength and power is directly proportional to the size of one's conference table. What is it about men and their dicks? Waving them around as though they are the most magnificent appendage in the known universe, rather than the scraggy-necked surplus skin hanging mostly limply atop a chap's even scraggier scrotum.

Women don't have this sort of metaphorical genital measuring competition. Our bits and bobs are neatly tucked inside. In fact, apocryphally, it is better for our sexual organs to be small and tight. Imagine that? A world where the man with the smallest cock rules the roost.

I don't really know where I'm going with this half-baked feminist rant and, by the time you have read it, International Women's Day will be over. Yes. A whole day for fifty per cent of the population to celebrate how far we have (or been allowed by men to have) come.

I'm gonna float away to Connie's world.

*** * ***

A Conference Table by Karl Whitmore

Table Talk by Ross Glanfield

It began with a poor recollection of history –
did Churchill wrap his riddle in an enigma or a mystery?
The contest that followed was witty and clever,
which of us could dream up the best conundrum ever.

You said: some things seem normal but verge on the weird,
such as how come Tarzan doesn't sport a beard?
I pondered on a commonplace paradox:
that perennial pair of unmatched socks.
You insisted minus one's square root is a quirk.
I wondered how snow plough drivers drove to work
then questioned whether Bigfoot has only got one leg?
You stooped to the obvious: chicken or egg?
We debated the best thing before *Mother's Pride*
and how come a football team is called a side?
Which is the smaller: soupcon or smidgeon?
And why do we never get to see baby pigeons?
Shouldn't there be a verse before the dawn chorus?
Why is there not another word for *thesaurus*?
Is the nuclear solution fusion or fission?
Why is there only one Monopolies' Commission?
Would "Walkers" be in business if they burnt things to a crisp?
And who cruelly put the letter *s* into lisp?
Which way round do you hang a horse's shoe?
How do we research a subject that's called "new"?
Can divine creation live with natural selection?
Is the needle sterilised for a lethal injection?

Drained of dilemmas, we call it a draw.
Then I delve deep inside and dream up one more.
Surely, I'll win the day with this romantic coup:
my favourite conundrum of all time is you.

13 Victoria Road by Pat Murgatroyd

We're going home to see our little Sally, Sally-Anne

Mum sang as she swung my arm backwards and forwards
in time to the clack of her heels and slap of my sandals
on damp pavements along the High Street, down Park Road,
round a corner towards home. I didn't want to see Sally-Anne.

Mum had been all mine in the fuggy darkness of the flea pit,
cheap seats at the pictures. My neck ached from craning up
at the screen, head leaning on her arm. Wrapped in the magic
of Clark Gable, she absent-mindedly held me close.

In the interval, Myra Slee from Number 23 (morphed
from usherette to ice-cream lady) stood at the front, her tray
slung round her neck. Mum sparked up another cigarette,
pushed a shilling into my hand for *Kia-Ora* or a tub of vanilla.

In love with the darkness, despite the prickle of grimy plush
on my bare legs, I didn't want to leave, ever. I wanted
her hand smoothing my hair, forever. The National Anthem
dragged me to my feet, lifted and crowded me into the foyer.

High Street drizzle and Park Road gloom unspooled the magic.
I dragged my heels at the corner, savoured the last clasp
of her hand before she opened the door to Number 13 and Dad
placed my grizzling baby sister into Mum's waiting arms.

I Come From… by Andrew Butcher

I come from a broken family in Buckskin, Basingstoke.
I come from the weird wilds of the Isle of Wight.
I come from thousands of years of genetic mutation.

I come from salty seasides.
I come from the decade of grit and gunge.
I come from art and isolation.
I took my toys to the nearby woods and made bases with them.

I come from Basil Brush and the dumping ground.
I come from Pokémon and Jungle Run.
I come from Saturday mornings with Ant & Dec.

I come from thick ears and banged heads,
grazed knees and bruises.

I learnt to hide before you knew we were playing.

I come from chaos and violence,
shouting and silence.
I come from stress, addiction,
steel-toe cap boots and kicked in walls.

I pretended to fly,

to delay the fall.

Shoes In The Bottom Of The Wardrobe by Pat Murgatroyd

They breathe a sigh of relief
when my charity shop round-up's over.
De-cluttering is postponed.

Slinky strappy sandals, black boots
laced to the knee, stilettos, all settle back
like chorus girls in a retirement home.
Scarlet espadrilles, sling-backs
re-live the glory days.

I have no use for them,
haven't for years, truth be told.
My sensible, black, extra-wides
are by the front door, rubber gardening clogs
by the back, and slippers for indoors.

I think I might be holding on to have-beens
because they bring me back to life
more clearly than photographs…
and I could turn up my toes any day now
or kick up my heels at any moment.

Further Adventures Of The Little Box by Maggie Sawkins
(in memory of Vasko Popa's poem, *The Little Box)*

Dear Mr Popa
Since you are dead, I am writing
with news of *The Little Box.*

When we first met (as a preface to a book
on how to cobble up a poem) it was like
looking into the face of a smile.

In July *The Little Box* and I attended
an event at The Botanical Gardens.
Though we were placed between lines
from *Paradise Lost* and *The Song of Quoodle,*
and the wind made the microphone groan
and the paper shake, you'll be pleased
to hear we held our own.

After, as we sat back on the grass,
and *Naming of Parts* boomed through
the speakers, people came up to ask
about *The Little Box.* I explained
I didn't know what it meant only that
it made me smile.

Then yesterday this:
after a brainstorm brought nil response
from my session with the mentally ill,
I took out *The Little Box* and sifted
its emptiness into the silence.

When I looked up your words were resting
like butterflies along their shoulders,
and on each face was a smile.

Sleep tight, Mr Popa,
I'm taking good care of *The Little Box.*

In Conversation: Hillard Morley & Jean G-Owen

 When Hillard Morley read an abridged copy of *Pride and Prejudice* while still in primary school, her desire to become a novelist was born. She wrote for the theatre company Rough House and tried her hand at poetry during the 1990s while pursuing a rewarding career as a Drama and English teacher, but her dream finally bore fruit in 2016, when she left her job and became a full-time writer. She has since published in prestigious literary journals worldwide, was shortlisted for the Independent Arts 'Jot' Award, and won the OWT Short Fiction Prize 2018, among other accolades. Hillard's debut novel *The Shadowing of Combfoot Chase* was published in August 2022. She has just completed her latest novel, *Nothing Starts But Everything Begins*.

Welcome Hillard Morley to *The Figlet* interview. Why the novel over other writing forms?
The novel enables me to play with form and still have elevated, poetic language. It's always been poetry and prose to me. I don't like a sentence that doesn't trip off the tongue, that doesn't flow, that isn't well-phrased. Maybe that echoes back to Drama – my roots are spoken word and "voice".

I wish I were like Dylan Thomas. It's the voices, how language is used for aural effect. I love creating little phrases, smaller than vignettes. Just little pockets of a moment which hang together perfectly.

What is your writing process – are you outline, plot and plan, or more organic?
I'm a bit of both. I "start writing into the dark" to quote Philip Pullman, and then refine it, picking out what I want, which sparks other ideas, and more research. It's a layering process and takes years. The book I've just finished, for instance, has had several incarnations dating back to 2018.

It's like a garden – you keep chopping back until you've get the form you want.

What do you most enjoy about writing?

When I don't remember writing a line…as if I've tapped into something bigger than myself. Not my ego – it's beyond that. I love the idea the Romans had – the genius in the walls. Sometimes, when it's really hard, I'll talk to the walls and say: *come on genius, where are you, crack on.* It liberates me: if the genius is not there, it's not my fault; if the genius is there, I can't take too much credit. It stops me getting too up myself.

Is there anything about being a writer you don't like?

The lack of money! The fact that when you've written your work of genius, it has to be turned into a product. I am not in the least bit interested in marketing. I would give my eye teeth to hand that over to somebody else except that I won't compromise the work I write in order to get an agent. An agent is only going to make money when the writer starts making money. But the world must be missing out on amazing writers because agents won't take a risk. It's a shame that art is suffering for business.

Everybody likes "happily ever after". Fairy tales are partly to blame for that. We end with the wedding and you never see how tough the marriage is; that Cinderella is about to kill the Prince after three years. I wish she'd married the frog instead.

What has been frustrating for you as a novelist?

One person who reviewed *The Shadowing of Combfoot Chase* put "one star, not for me" and couldn't be bothered to say why. My publisher had pitched it as a thriller – which it is, and it isn't, in equal measure. Some readers complain that I don't give the ultimate answer at the end of that novel. It's frustrating when people want me to answer every question but are only prepared to read it once. I remember Ali Smith saying: "why do you think that you should read a book once and then you're done. You watch films multiple times, or you listen to songs over and over again…" – why would a novel be any different? Readers have this attitude that you read the book once, it should have a beginning, middle, and end, and then you're done. Whereas I want a deep dive into a text…not just a superficial skim through.

The novel is a young form of literature. I think that's what appeals to me in a way, because we're still pushing boundaries of what it can do. Drama has always been so much more ready to shoot everything up and throw everything in the air. I think part of me just wants to take a sledgehammer to the conventional novel.

Some readers only want tradition – resolution. I mean, there are many experimental novels that readers either like or not. I guess that's how it is for The Shadowing of Combfoot Chase?
Combfoot combines the incredibly contemporary with echoes of tradition. We never know who's watching us. It's about fear, discomfort, uncertainty, and it's political. My husband described it as like standing in an art gallery and looking at a series of paintings on the wall…you stand in the middle of a room of images and are invited to make connections.

The language is beautiful, and readable but you have to stay on your game. That makes for active participation in the reading process, what you call "the deep dive".
I don't have the patience to write in any other way. If I haven't got that hook to pull me deep, I can't spend the time with it myself.

That's the kind of reader you want, isn't it – someone who's prepared to put their hook in, which brings us to your latest novel Nothing Starts But Everything Begins. Could you tell me something about it?
It is set in one hour in a dismal Midland town. Five years ago a girl died and the members of her family have been scarred by that death and flung apart. For various reasons they are now coming back together. In some ways it's a ghost story, in others it uses the metaphor of a ghost to explore whether you're the type of person who gets stuck in the past, whether you can pull what's good from the past and move it forwards, or whether you just disregard it.

This is not your Turn of the Screw, ghost stalking. The ghost is there and you can believe in her if you wish, as a presence, or you can say she's just a metaphor, a representation of the memory of her. So there's lots about memory, dust, and the fact that nothing ever goes away, that we're just recycled.

That certainly is a deep dive and a fascinating topic. I wish you all the best on your publication journey. Have any odd writing habits?
Is it odd that I have a strict routine. I am a morning person and get to my desk by 9:00 at the latest. I don't move until a good day's work has been done. In that first phase of writing, I stay at my desk until I've written a thousand words. Other odd habits: I drink water, I eat some chocolate – good dark chocolate.

No wonder you get things finished! What do you think you bring to the Isle of Wight as a writer?
I hope aspiration, you know, that actually the world's a bigger place. Because it's very easy to write bucolic pieces about hills and trees in a world that's about to explode. There are more important things to consider. That's why I'm so fascinated by this idea of dust – that everything comes from dust and that's where we're heading again. There's a lot of that in the latest book, hence the title. I think we on the Isle of Wight writing scene can be a bit complacent. I would like to think that I tackle something a bit more global, maybe.

On that optimistic note, Hillard Morley, it's been an absolute pleasure talking with you. Thank you.

https://www.bookguild.co.uk/authors/author-detail/1394/

Ethel by Hillard Morley

Ethel would not wear her glasses
(in spite of being an optician).
I thought her false
and hated her for it.

She took too many risks and
put my favourite puppet in a teapot.
"Just call me Ethel," she requested,
(detested being "Aunty" as it made her feel too old).

I could not do it.
I found the very thought
too daring and informal.

She was the only person I had met
who possessed a tambourine.
She would bang it viciously
whilst shouting out: 'A Love Song'
sung to Jesus.

She told me a rude joke about a pansy
and asked if I would paint her.
She bought the canvas and the oils
(which I had no idea how to use)
and when I made a wave,
she shrieked: "An Abstract! Just the ticket!"

I should have loved someone
who could be brave enough to be
so unconventional,
but I could not forgive her courage
and I hung onto my rage.

Silence by Maggie Sawkins

It's not the kind that whips its tail
against the heart and makes you wonder
    what ill you've done;

not the kind that sets up home
between the ears or drones in the blood
until you no longer can hear the man
    on the radio or the cat's meow;

it's not the kind that broods well
into the night, so that even between
the sheets, the words you're trying to read
    lift from the page like a swarm –

it's not the kind whose off switch,
though so close, is out of reach –
    no, it's not that kind of silence.

Mastermind by Yvonne Brown

Was I your ultimate goal?
A prize to be competed for?

Others were seeking my affection –

I chose you – sat in your big, black, leather armchair
answering my questions
with a confident, self-assured air.

(Charm being your specialist subject).

You passed on one or two.
The awkward questions you didn't care to answer.
Don't bother to deny it.
No – "I've started, so I'll finish".

I must have been a fool
to believe in your sense of fair play

for, once the prize was won
you went on to other competitions,
masterminding your plan
to win the love of another innocent.

The Wall Of Love by Heather Whatley

Kelly sat cross-legged on the floor of her bedsit putting the finishing touches to her wall of love. She was surrounded by photographs of him: newspaper clippings, holiday photos, celebrations. They all showed the same engaging smile of the married man she was obsessed with.

Selecting another photo, which had two happy people in it, she cut around the shape with the utmost care and sighed as the scissors slid around his form. The sensual movement of her fingers around the beloved figure of Brian Whitely was contrasted by the sudden, snapping of the blades as she severed his smiling wife away from his side. Then, with Brian's shape between her fingers, she lifted him reverently to take his place beside her in one of the many creations.

Thus Kelly Stobbs and Brian Whitely were conjoined. The careful choreography of the photos and her obsession with him, married in her mind to create a reality, if not a legality.

She stepped back to admire her work. The walls of her bedsit were covered with similar fantasy testimonies to their love: Brian and Kelly on the beach in Tenerife; Brian blowing kisses to her; happy parties. She had even engineered a photo of them side-by-side at Christmas time – that pinnacle of loving togetherness. And in every photo his eyes seemed to sparkle with love for only her – another feat of modern technology.

A shard of reality shot through Kelly as she remembered the discarded wife. A knot of jealous rage bunched inside her. She grabbed the fruit knife and stabbed it repeatedly into the serene, impassive face of Mrs. Jayne Whitely, pockmarking her flawless complexion. She crumpled the distorted image inside her angry fists until her white knuckles almost burst through her skin. As a finale to this outburst she created a pyre in her saucepan, sneering as the face melted into oblivion.

"Now we're completely alone," Kelly whispered to her wall of love.

Exhausted by her preparations and her rage, she sunk back on the golden, velvet cushions she had stolen from Brian's home, content that the other woman was out of the picture.

Northernhay Gardens by Tim Cooper

I don't know why she's brought me to the park
just to fight. I mean, it's May.
The sun is shining, cherry bloom and stuff.

I don't even know what she's cross about
except everything I say
seems to make it worse and people are starting to stare.

Eventually, I've had enough. I snap
and walk away.
She brings my shabby logic back

to where she is
for there it is
ris-ing
    turn-ing
fall-ing
    bounc-ing
the ring, the ring, the ring.
The *everything-I-owned-which-I-sold-to-buy-her-a-ring* ring
is now stuck between two blades of grass
over where the council mower passed
an hour ago, not lost, just hard to find.

Fighting for foibles, squabbles in the park,
lovers do these things as concrete markers
against the fear they have that passion is temporary,
love an illusion, and so for the next hour,
as I pace the park looking
each bent blade of grass I tread down becomes something,
a part of the path,
a concrete reminder –
the story of how we became.

Death And The Maiden by Jean G-Owen

In the late 1990s, a friend introduced me to a nineteenth-century poem by Matthias Claudius titled 'Der Tod und Das Mädchen' ['Death and the Maiden']. The idea of death personified as a skeleton seducing a maiden to her untimely end developed from the Medieval 'Dance of Death', a popular motif in Renaissance Art, and later with the likes of artist Edvard Munch.

I wasn't much impressed with the many English translations of the original poem so my friend challenged me to compose a version of my own despite the fact that my knowledge of German is rudimentary. The two poems – by Matthias Claudius and my own version – appear in my poetry collection *Bites of Love: Poems & Images*. Both feature here, along with an amusing illustration by Karl Whitmore.

Der Tod Und Das **Mädchen**

Das Mädchen:
Vorüber! Ach, Vorüber!
Geh, wilder Knochenmann!
Ich bin noch jung! Geh! Lieber!
Und rühre mich nicht an.

Der Tod:
Gib deine Hand, du schön und zart Gebilde!
Bin Freund und komme nicht zu strafen.
Sei gutes Muts! Ich bin nicht wild,
Sollst sanft in meinen Armen schlafen!

The Maiden Gives Death the Finger by Karl Whitmore

Death And The Maiden

The Maiden:
Sod off! Sod off!
You bony, brittle man.
You're old and rough,
I've had enough.
I know your fiendish plan!

Death:
Don't play hard to get with me
You fair and feisty form.
Come over here, lie my arms,
I'll keep you safe and warm.
I'm not a perv; I'm your best friend.
Why resist me? You'll be mine in the end.

Snobbery In A Graveyard by Pat Murgatroyd

A flagstone path from lychgate to church door is a ley-line
straight as a bookmark in the heavy Bible's spine inside.
It divides old graveyard from new, ancient from modern.
Stone sepulchres on one side, family tombs, private
as a bishop's wife, they exude wealth, privilege, power.
Lichened memorials stand smug inside ivy-swagged railings.
On the other side stretch orderly rows of marble headstones,
gold lettering, grey gravel. Respectful, seemly flowerpots.

Today's dead are in the "new" cemetery, graves cluttered
with paraphernalia, *let it all out* grief (I blame Lady Di).
Burdened by glass chippings the colour of swimming pools,
they're laden with photos, teddy bears, fake unseasonal blooms.
I prefer the cold dignity of old Lord Bathurst's plot, looking down
on me, to the vulgarity of plastic tulips and football scarves.

They Are Gone by Sandy Kealty

Through the rooms, the neighbours drift and totter, pick and poke.
It makes a change from squabbling and measuring the grass.

They had some good stuff.

An A-board prominent on the driveway: *Estate Sale Here Today!*
It makes a change from shopping at the mall or eating cake.

They had some good stuff.

This is how they do it here in California.
They don't anonymise the process at an auction.
They empty all the cupboards, all the garage shelves
and lay the bounty out in sad, vacated rooms
for sale by Liquidation Services, qualified to maximise returns.

They had some good stuff.

Through the rooms the neighbours cruise and amble, reminisce.
It makes a change from pickleball and gazing through the window.

They had some good stuff.

Furniture with curves and curls, embarrassment of handles,
ginger jars, boxed cigars, linen, mostly clean, unused for years,
china animals, all ranked in herds.
There are no words for this conspicuous exposure.

"I do this most weekends,"
                    a woman with a lip-sticked smile informs us.
"I live just round the corner, but I didn't know them well.
They had some good stuff."

In the hall, a bland-faced overseer counts the dimes and quarters.
I buy two candle sticks and a pretty plate.
There's a twenty-five per cent reduction, as it's Sunday.
"You should have been here yesterday. They had some good stuff."

In the closet hangs a sagging velvet jacket, and a dressing gown.
On the bedside table, two half-empty bottles – gin, I think –
a photo frame, a bowl of plastic beads.

I have no notion who they were. They had some good stuff.

Memories by Lisa Scovell-Strickland

Memories old and new, fade together
Hidden through time, perhaps forever
I can't distinguish the beginning from the end
What's past, present, future, I can't comprehend
There are snippets and flashbacks, of black and white
Like an old movie film that is wound too tight
The film has snapped, the memories lost
But the editor is pasting, at no extra cost
The final scene is being replaced
It's now the beginning, he's run out of paste
Locked up for now, the keys can't be found
The memory is intact, waiting around
They wait for me, they wait for you
They are waiting 'til old becomes new

The Darkness Of Your Eyes by Lisa Scovell-Strickland

My fragile existence trapped
on the edge of greatness
I'm blinded by emptiness
hidden under a broken wing
longing for a white flag
wishing upon a fallen star
sight in my mind's eye
clouded in pain everlasting

I searched for you in the light of your smile
but lost me in the darkness of your eyes

When I Am Blind, I Shall Not... by Kate Young

write in colour. I shall not say
the sky is steel-grey, or marvel how
scarlet forests stand on smoky hills.
I shall not declare the sea is blue,
or that your eyes are tawny brown.
Instead, I shall measure your warmth
with my fingertips on your cheek.
Or feel the icy blue curl of
an autumn's wave on my toes
and sense the chill of deepening shadows
as I walk under the foot of the cliffs.
I shall hear the crunch of leaves
under my feet in the forest,
and smell the damp moss and earth.
Feel the steepness of the hill in
my laboured breath and rising pulse.
Taste frying bacon on the air –
or hear sausages sizzling in the pan.
Sense you settle in the chair beside me,
and know my value by the closeness of you.

Drowned by Annys Brady

"You have a little girl now?" I asked.
All light tone and lighter smile.

Your eyes, like stars in an ocean,
betrayed you.

"Yes, I do," you said.

(To replace the boy I lost)

You didn't say.

In that moment,
next to packets of rice, jam jars and coffee biscuits

words hung empty like brittle bones
and I wondered how you had
drowned all these years

without dying.

Ebbing by Kate Young

White walls whizzing by –
the antiseptic smell, fears
choke my throat.

We knew this would happen
born with an imperfect heart,
my brother, born to die.

Why at only three?
His whole life before him –
and I just a year older.

I'm told to sit outside,
night slides by, mum and dad
return to hold my hand.

In the back of the car
there is now an empty seat
which won't be filled.

The curving coastal road
whisks us away from there –
the dark sea sweeps by.

In my ears the roar
of the ebbing tide –
time and tide won't turn back.

At home in the starlit garden,
my parents stand close, yet apart.

YARNIVAL 2024

WEST WIGHT WORDFEST

FRI 27—SAT 28 SEPTEMBER

Walk & Write in Tennyson's Footsteps

Verbal & Sound Artists' Performances

Storytelling for Children

Songwriting Workshop

Scriptwriting Workshop

'From the Heart' Poetry Recital

Writers' Roundtable

Book Fair

Naked Figleaf Press

Poet-Tree

Booking Essential

We Give A Fig

jean28owen@gmail.com

Yarnival 2024 Draft Programme

Friday 27 September	Venue	Event
Jean G-Owen & Steve Taverner	Freshwater Bay 12:30-3:30	Walk & Write in Tennyson's Footsteps
A Wealth of Words hosted by Jean G-Owen	CHOYD, Yarmouth 7:00-10:00 pm Tickets £5.00	Wordsmiths & Sound Artists Performance Evening

Saturday 28 Sept	Venue	Event
Children's Storytelling with Holly Medland, Sue Clark & Merl Fluin	Freshwater Library 10:00-11:30 Free Event Booking Essential	Join members of the Island Storytellers to help the mermaid find her tail, cook up a story & have fun monkeying around.
Scriptwriting Workshop with Cheryl May	The Wheatsheaf, Yarmouth 10:00-12:00 Free Event Booking essential	Explore techniques of writing a ten-minute play: structure, character, plot, & audience expectations.
Songwriting Workshop with Ross Westrop	CHOYD 10:00-12:00 Free Event Booking essential	Write a song in two hours using techniques such as building a story, hooks, tune, & melody.
'From the Heart' Poetry Recital with Maggie Sawkins & Jean G-Owen	CHOYD 2:00-3:00 Free Event Pledge essential	Pledge to learn a published poem (not your own) & recite it in front of an audience.
Writers' Roundtable chaired by Jean G-Owen	CHOYD 3:20-4:00 All welcome at this free event	Join IOW writers Cheryl May, Maggie Sawkins & Anmarie Bowler in a lively discussion about writing on the Island.
Spoken Word Finale hosted by Graham Brown	CHOYD 4:15-5:15	Poets and spoken word artists gather for the Yarnival Finale.

Who Do You See? by J. W. Edge

Who do you see when you look at me?
Do you see the happy-go-lucky kid
who once tried everything? Yes, I did!
Or the graceful slip of a girl who caught the eye
of many a stranger or friend passing by.
Or the woman whose strength supported all,
who stood for justice, who stood tall.
Do you see the woman
who collected knowledge and skill?
The woman who worked, commanded respect until...
in later years worked her art and sang her song,
who to community did belong?
Do you see the pain behind the eyes?
The loss of a sister, the loss of a child,
or the crippling pain from all the breaks,
the muscle spasms, the constant aches?
Or do you see an empty shell?
Just another being with no tale to tell,
sometimes pitied, but oh, so old,
a passing phase that will not hold.
No mark upon your youth,
am I of no consequence or truth?
Well, let me tell you, when the day is done,
here in time be you, when I am gone.

Brined by Ian Winter

All we can hear is the heat.

It buzzes past in insect clouds.
It drops to our ears in the beat
of impossibly heavy pelican wings,
and scratchily pulses
from the dwindle-bodied sand-critters
of this equatorial beach.

Shimmering,
the sound shrouds this sun-bleached sheet
of tropical sand,
where you stand,
with your toes in the tickling fingers
of surf's frothy hand.

Left and right on the strand,
in the sea, on the land,
not a soul breaks the haze.
Sunlight strobes from the waves,
as you splashily pace –
under-glow on your face –
at peace, with yourself,
with this beautiful place.

I'm sitting, I'm distant,
I wait, I'm in shade,
blissfully watching your bare-footed wade
as we both fantasise
that we can live free,
where the sea
meets the sky
meets the coconut tree.

You May Cause A Swell To Happen by Ellie Roddick

You may cause a swell to happen,
but allow it to run to the shore without pushing.
Either to fall away,
or to reach its own perfect conclusion at the turn,
unaided by your rushing.

Set in motion what you will,
but let the tide take it forward
as you float in the stream,
unconcerned for how and where and when, or even if,
the swell will reach the pebbled beach you dream of.

Scar On The Rock by Steve Taverner

Two facts about limpet life that are vital to understanding the following poem: firstly, limpets start life as boys and grow into women. For those of you who like big words, this process is known as being a protandrous hermaphrodite. The second fact is that, in order to avoid drying out when the tide is out, limpets clamp down firmly to the rock in the same place every time, eventually forming a mark on the rock called a home scar. [S.T.]

Lucy the limpet had lived a long time,
a venerable mollusc, now well past her prime.
As a boy she'd discovered this rock smooth and flat
with plenty of algae to help him grow fat.
So she'd stay here forever, reluctant to move,
and into the rock she'd worn a deep groove.

As for family, though to us it might seem somewhat sad,
she'd no notion to whom she'd been mother or dad,
for they'd all drifted off to far distant shores
or ended their lives between hungry jaws.

Ten thousand tides she had seen come and go,
her hard hat protecting her from every foe.
But now she was weak and could hold on no more,
and so a huge wave washed her clean off the shore.
Her time it was over, she'd run down the clock,
and all that was left was a scar on the rock.

For us, too, the clock ticks and ticks all too fast
though we cling to our rock, we know it can't last.
When my time is over, when there's no more Steve,
I wonder what manner of scar I might leave.

Will it be poetry, or students inspired
to study the seashore, more limpets admired.
Or will no-one know that I've lived and I've died
and care not a jot for all that I've tried?

It's foolish to worry, for scars seldom last,
erosion soon sees they're consigned to the past.
So don't think of your scar, just enjoy yourself now,
before your time comes to take that last bow.

SATIRICAL WIT & VULGAR VERSE

by STEVE TAVERNER

Steve Taverner began his comic poetry career to entertain biology A-level students while working as a field studies teacher. He has since branched out to write on a variety of topics with an emphasis on light entertainment. *Star on the Rock*, Steve's debut collection of satirical wit and vulgar verse, was published by Naked Figleaf Press in 2024.

https://nakedfigleafcollective.co.uk/scar-on-the-rock/

Rhythms by Andrew Butcher

The ocean sees us dancing,
feels the ebb and flow of our swaying
as we work out each other's rhythms,
as you work out the world through your bright little eyes
and I work through the pain behind mine.

The grass salutes us,
standing tall, telling us it will always be there beneath our feet
as we explore the world for the first time, together.

The sun shines down on us,
showering us with light and hope, brightening our days,
helping us leave the darkness behind, even for just a moment.

For the only moment that matters is here and now, with you,
as we search the world for meaning through generations of difference.
I love you,
and I will do everything I can to protect you.   Always.

For I may not know how to do this yet, but I can learn.
I want us to find these rhythms together,
to make new melodies that last forever.

Please know that I did all I could.
Even when times were tough, I tried my best.
And yes, I wasn't always good at this,
but how can anyone be perfect at something they've never done?

You are the world   and I am your rock.
Currently keeping you anchored.
One day weighing you down.

After all, that's what parents do eventually,
even without realising.

The ocean is shrouded in misty unknown.
It cannot feel our rhythms anymore.

Albion, Awake From Your Slumber by Eric Ferris

A footfall echoes in a wooded glade.
Dark eyes glisten in a sea of jade.
From the centre of gloom rears an ugly tree,
a victim of its age and history.

A jet-black raven is drawn to the sound,
bird's head twisting, searching around.
Fledglings cry pitifully, can closed eyes see?
As the raven flies on to its deity.

The tree's branches shiver, a bass voice speaks,
it stutters and stinks in emaciated cheeks.
A high-pitched scream comes from every plant.
The corpse of a weasel begins to chant:
"There's a lank, cowled figure with a wizened hand
spreading doom-like prophecies throughout our land."

Wild wind and rain add to the tumult,
will raven swear allegiance to the cult?
Circling twice, past Dorset's west moors,
then spiralling down to the New Forest's floor.

Young babies cried angrily. What could they see?
As brave raven flew steadily on to me.
In the year of Our Lord, twenty-twenty-four,
I plucked this script from a raven's claw:

"Oh Albion, awake from your slumber,
at your door evil hosts without number.
When England's cities are frozen in snow,
alas, too late then to arrest the flow.'

A lank, cowled figure with a wizened hand,
spreading doom-like prophecies throughout our land.
With courage now, take a warrior's path,
or our children's future will haunt our hearts.

Albion, Be Still In Your Slumber by Eric Ferris

A clear voice echoes in a wooded glade.
Bright eyes glisten in a sea of jade.
From the centre of light spreads a wondrous tree,
a tribute to its age and history.

A flawless dove rejoices at the sound,
bird's head joyfully questing around.
Fledglings cry happily, can closed eyes see?
As the dove flies on to its deity.

The tree's branches quiver, the panpipes speak,
fauns hither and thither with puffed-red cheeks.
Melodious tunes sound from every plant,
as fairies and pixies begin to chant:
"There's a fresh new prophet with a healing hand,
spreading joyful stories throughout our land."

Soft breeze and sun calm any tumult,
will dove swear allegiance to the cult?
Circling twice, past Devon's charmed moors,
gyrating down to Glastonbury's Tor.

Young babies laugh excitedly. What can they see?
As brave dove flies steadily on to me.
In the year of Our Lord, twenty-twenty-four,
I plucked this script from a white dove's claw:

"Oh Albion, be still in your slumber,
at your door fortune smiles on your number.
When England's cities bathe in crystals of snow,
come one, come all to the enchanted flow.

A fresh new prophet with a healing hand,
spreading wonderful stories throughout our land.
With clarity now, take a pacifist's path,
or our children's future will haunt our hearts.

Ukraine Woe by Norman Figueiredo

This war of attrition brings misery
as the Russian troops invade an independent nation.

Young, inexperienced men
are conscripted on both sides.

Peace talks are stalled.

Russian troops take advantage
by bombing strategic positions around Kyiv.

Civilians bombed, made homeless.

Evacuees flee their homes to seek refuge
in neighbouring countries such as Poland.

The despotic Putin and his army prove to be a mighty force
against the Ukraine minnows.

The US supply cluster bombs to Ukraine,
but they may cause civilian casualties in this warfare.

Battle fatigue among soldiers on both sides prevails.

The UN fear there may be an escalation in the conflict,
leading to a war in Europe.

Putin knows he's committed war crimes in Ukraine.
Let us not forget them when this conflict ends.

Nuclear tactical weapons are primed and armed.
Let us hope and pray this does not become reality.

Anywhere But Here by Peter May

An old friend who did his national service in the Royal Artillery, related this tale. If by chance it should be read by an old gunner, the story is true, but the details and military procedures may not be accurate.

In a muddy field, somewhere in Germany, there was a small battery of twenty-five pounder field guns, each with its crew of six gunners. Mostly young conscripts, all were wishing they were somewhere else. Crowded around the gun, awaiting the order to fire, each man in his designated position, trained for a specific task. The gun squatted solidly between them. Big. Ugly. Rampant. It was spotless, cleaned, oiled, polished. The gun had become the centre of their world. Revered, almost sacred, on occasion, saluted.

The order came: "Fire!"

Nothing.

Then again: "Fire!"

It was a misfire. For some reason, the fuse or charge had failed to ignite. The shell could explode at any time, putting the gun in jeopardy. The gunmaster or – 'ACK. I.G.' – was called.

He confirmed the misfire and gave the order: "To the rear of the gun."

This required the shell to be removed from the breech and taken to a position at least fifty yards from the gun. A man was called forward. He scooped up the shell, turned and started across the field. He was half a stride into a run when someone shouted:

"Walk! Don't shake the bloody thing."

Jimmy Smith, known as Smiffy to his friends, was nineteen years old and lived in a small northern town with his widowed mother. He had a reasonable job with the prospects of a promotion and a pension at the end. At weekends he would cheer on his local football team, drink beer and spend time with his friends. Life was good. Until that day in 1953 when, in a muddy field, he was ordered to carry an unexploded shell to safety.

Under his breath he repeated: "Don't shake it, don't shake it." He walked straight-legged as fast as he could, with the shell held at arms-length in front of him. But it was too heavy, his arms might shake. Clutching it to his chest felt safer. Could he hear it ticking or fizzing or was that the sound of blood pounding in his ears? He glanced back over his shoulder, the gun seemed far enough away. Bending down he put the shell carefully on the ground, but it was on a small mound and rolled over before coming to a halt. A sudden moment of fear gripped Jimmy in the stomach like a cold hand. His knees gave way and he fell backward on to the ground. Jumping to his feet, he turned and ran towards the gun. Halfway back, he decided that the shell was not going to explode. He slowed to a casual saunter, and then a swagger.

"Alright, Smiffy?" said a voice.

"Yeah, piece of cake."

Our Pet Mother by Maggie Sawkins

If only she would come down
from the mountain and be
like one of the chinchillas
Mr Chapman spent eleven years coaxing,
we would wrap her in iced black sheets
just like he did
until she got used to the sun.

Then we would build a cage
right here in our bedroom
tempt her with titbits of roots,
alfalfa and bark,
give her a tray of white sand
to keep her cool.

Each night we'd promise
to lift up the latch,
let her hop onto the carpet
and watch as she ricocheted
from wall to wall.

Then we would catch her and cup her
in the palms of our hands
sink our fingers
into her plush grey fur
and feel her quiver. She'd be
so, so soft we would almost drown.

Red Squirrels by Jamie Britton

Watch Dog Alert by Cheryl May

The term watchdog conjures up
some delightfully absurd images.
Imagine if you will…

Droolius Caesar, a slobbering mastiff
watching a pot that never boils.

Tortellini, a twitching terrier, all a-flutter,
binoculars at the ready for a spot of birdwatching.

Bramble, a rather sheepish border collie
having the wool pulled over her eyes.

Kevin, a King Charles spaniel with a cavalier attitude to life,
curled up on the couch watching a dogumentary on TV.

Winnie the poodle,
a dog star in her own right, observing the sky at night.

Brandy, a barrel-shaped Saint Bernard,
watching his weight.

Peter the pointer,
tail and foreleg raised, head extended,
pointing his muzzle at a quivering quarry.

Spiv, a strapping Great Dane, legs festooned
with Timex, Seiko, Omega and Rolex –
the definitive watch dog.

In Memoriam Of Benny, The Cockerel by Tim Cooper

who was killed by a fox despite his loud protestations that this could not be tolerated but which, regrettably, woke me too late to do anything about it.

There is no love in my cockerel.
He is *glad* when the hens spend the night in his house
or roost on the branches beneath him,
but he killed his brother for this privilege
and that's hard to forgive.

His joyless cries each morning
serve only to oppress the egos of those who might stand
against him. "Cock-uck-a-fuck-you-all,"
he shouts at the sun, then turns on the hens.
"You're all bitches and ho's."

Entering his run he comes at you,
like pub-car-park boxer, easy to mock
if you're not directly involved. I'd swing my boot
at him, but my wife, she picks him up in her arms.
"Oh, Benny, my love, you're so silly," she says.

Dark fire and hatred dart from his eyes
but he cannot resist.
Love, in the end, comes to Benny.

Metamorphosis by Julie Watson

(With apologies to Kafta)

There is a slim gap between the drawn curtains. A ray of morning sunshine has slipped inside and is creeping slowly over the duvet dunes towards me. I'm lying curled like a comma in my warm nest. I extend one arm, then the other, greeting the morning with a stretch of my upper spine and a wide yawn. A glance at the clock tells me – not yet. My bed is seductively warm and soft. I settle my head on my hands again.

But my eyes do not close. My stomach is growling for breakfast. No cereal today; I crave something fishy. Some kippers, perhaps.

And I'll skip my morning shower. The very idea of getting wet strikes me as repugnant today. Why do we need to ablute ourselves? The Elizabethans went for months without a bath. I press my nose to my arm, inhale the scent and impulsively give it a quick lick to be sure. I'm clean enough.

One further spinal stretch, and then it's time. Slipping out feet first, I feel for my sheepskin slippers and step forward but immediately stumble, falling onto my hands on the carpet. I try to stand but somehow can't get upright on my feet. My back refuses to straighten, so I opt for a quadrupedal trot into the kitchen instead.

There, I sit on the floor to consider the situation. My thoughts are interrupted by the raucous noise assaulting my ears. It's coming from the garden – an insufferable cacophony of twittering birds squabbling around the feeders. Distressing for my poor ears. I will cover them, but as I do so, I discover something unexpected. I never realised, until now, quite how silky they feel. I stroke each of them in turn, then touch the tips. Curiously, they feel rather pointy today, Spock-like, in fact.

With growing unease, I crouch on the kitchen floor, flexing my hands instinctively to calm myself. Then: alarm bells! These are not my hands but someone else's. Fingers, which once tapered elegantly down to manicured nails, have coalesced into round pads. And every nail has turned into a lethal-looking hook of keratin.

Something else has happened overnight. The skin that covers my hands and feet has sprouted hair – a thick black pelt of the stuff. Fear takes hold, and my mouth turns dry. Pushing up my pyjama top, I see that this furry growth extends over my stomach. I reach up to my face. Yes, there, too.

Then, a strange swishing sound comes from behind me. I spin around and see a long black tail lashing the kitchen floor unhappily as it disappears from view. And horror of horrors – it's attached to me! This is too much. I open my mouth, but no scream comes out. Instead, a strangulated yowl. It can't be, but it sounds like…a meow. It is. With a shock, I now understand. I have turned into a cat.

Witch by Graham Brown

According to the neighbours
Mrs Mulheron is a witch.
When she cursed last summer
it rained non-stop
from Whitsun to Michaelmas.

One by one, the children disappeared.
They tell me all this between cups of coffee.
I smile politely as I close the door.

These packing boxes won't empty themselves.

The estate agent's brochure
Makes no mention of Wicca in the area.

I'm sure the butcher's van
outside Mrs Mulheron's
is for that odd, yellow-eyed cat
staring from her veranda.

I think I'll fit in nicely around here.

Ziggy by Becky Haydock

SPLISH! SPLASH! SLODGE!

Oh! Ziggy
I wish you could dodge
   those great, big, dirty puddles

as you leave
     your feline footprints
         across the clean sheets of my new diary.

Really, oh really, Ziggy?

I write how I love him, but now I'm not so sure
     as he curls up and purrs
         deeply, softly on my lap

Extra cuddles for you, my love…
before you start all over again
       tomorrow
    with those big, muddy paws!

Ziggy by Tina Goode

Pawprint by Diana Kimpton

Halfway up the back wall of our house is a pawprint. Just one. It looks as if it was made by a cat – a cat with only one leg. Or maybe it was made by a fleet-footed, agile cat who hurtled down our garden, threw itself into the air and hit our wall with just one paw before it plummeted down to earth, landing neatly on all four feet like cats do.

It's more likely that the print belonged to an adventurous cat – one determined to explore the fresh-made bricks waiting to be baked. A cat who, acting as if it had every right to be there, marched arrogantly from one brick to another, leaving a footprint in each one – left fore, left hind, right fore, right hind – a trail that horrified the brickmaker when he returned from lunch.

Unwilling to start again, he baked them anyway, then mixed the damaged bricks with the good ones – one per load. So our house has one footprint halfway up the wall as a testament to that cat's audacity, while somewhere, there must be other houses whose owners are wondering about the existence of one-legged cats.

Spider by Chris Rickards

All night I laboured
spinning
spinning
my gossamer thread

How I ached
yet could not stop
compelled by nature's need to
spin
spin
spin

I spin for my food
I spin for my safety
I spin for creation
for eternal procreation
for the perpetuity
of my kind

For beauty
for subtle sound
as a gentle breeze
whispers through my threads
and diamond dew-drops
become rainbows

Humankind
marvel
at the intricate artistry
of my work

Mr Figgy, mascot of Naked Figleaf Collective, by Karl Whitmore

The inaugural Isle of Wight Biosphere Festival coincided with the launch of this issue of *The Figlet*, so what better way to celebrate our island's UNESCO biosphere reserve status than with the featured theme "Footprints". In this vibrant section of the magazine, twenty writers and illustrators address what has become a critical topic in politics, as much as in prose and poetry, as we face the effects our actions have on our planet.

Of particular note is Cat James' acerbic article 'There Is No Planet B', in which she confronts the issue of how we should rethink the primary sector of production as much as its end products. Emily Gillatt-Ball's poignant childhood memory of Alum Bay weaves nostalgia with history, and Felicity Fair Thompson's touching piece remembers Exercise Tiger, the D-Day rehearsal on Slapton Sands.

Other writings consider footprints in terms of what remains as much as what is lost forever through topics such as love, time, longing, sea- and landscape, and dinosaurs. I hope you enjoy reading this selection as much as I did.

Three Sets Of Footprints by Karl Whitmore

One: 125 Million Years Ago

A creature whose name I cannot pronounce
makes its marks down Yaverland way.
Today, the prints are still on the beach
and the skeleton is on display.

Two: 1969

An astronaut's boot in the lunar soil
is visible to this day,
to remain on the moon for a million years
with nothing to erode it away.

Three: 2024

Muddy wellingtons on the hall carpet.
I just went outside to play.
Mum scrubs the stains and says bad words.
It's not fair is it, eh?

There Is No Planet B by Cat James

Sometimes, I think I must sound like a dreary old gubber, a throwback of a bygone age. And I'm not alone; a fan wrote of my article about Robin Askwith: "This belongs in the 70s, leave it there!" However, I believe that the solution to the world's ills can be found in the television of my seventies youth.

For those of you old enough to remember, the 1970s may be the decade you'd rather forget.

Sure, we had power cuts, smoking in pubs and offensive comedians, but there was also Women's Lib, the litter-hating Wombles – and short documentaries viewed through the arched window.

And it is these little films that may hold the answer to today's profligate society and our single-use disposable attitude. Via those presentations, wide-eyed children (and adults) could see how things were made. A trip to a bottling plant, with freshly sterilised glass containers jingle-jangling their way along a conveyor belt to be refilled with milk. A man working a lathe, turning the spindles for a chair, having first chosen his wood; the creation of a piece of furniture shown from raw material to finished product.

A decade or so later I trained as an industrial designer and, as I went on a tour around an injection-moulding factory with my fellow students, I watched in awe as tiny plastic beads were fed into a hopper before being heated, squirted into a steel mould and spat out the other end as a yoghurt carton. So, with all this manufacturing insight, I studied seasonal electrical items in *Poundland* in the run up to that festival of commerce – Hallowe'en – and despaired at how these trinkets were sold for a mere quid before being presumably consigned to the bin on their journey to landfill.

Deep in Russia's Kupol mine, north of the Arctic Circle and 140 miles away from the nearest town, workers endure extreme conditions to bring gold to the surface. Gold is used in smartphones. The raw materials for batteries include steel and zinc. Plastic is made from oil, itself created naturally from decaying prehistoric plant and animal remains. These metals and other elements are the earth's precious – and finite – resources, which are relentlessly recovered in variable conditions all around the world.

That packet of pumpkin lights which I saw in *Poundland* was not made by elves. Oil, metal and wood were used in its manufacture; its components assembled on the other side of the world then shipped across the oceans for us to buy one day and chuck away the next.

Did those prehistoric animals die for this? The solution is more fundamental than sanctimoniously refusing a plastic straw in your drink. We have lost sight of how things are made; not understanding the expenditure of natural and human resources that go into glittery pens, gimmicky fairy lights, and other unnecessary tat.

Instead of thinking how we can 'recycle' our unwanted stuff, let's consider how it was made – and if it should be made, and bought, at all.

Moving On by Peter May

Dear J.C

I'm sorry to have to inform you by letter but seeing you hasn't been possible since the trial. I have decided to leave the disciples. I've always found it tough going, walking miles, following you everywhere, living on handouts, and suffering constant insults and attacks, not to mention the number of footprints we all leave. For what? A promise of something good after I'm dead?

I have had enough. It's all different now. I've met someone. You remember that woman you saved from stoning? Well, we've been seeing each other and intend to get married. We think we can make a go of things with plans for a small business in outside catering. You must remember feeding the five thousand. It's like that but on a smaller scale. She's got a little money put aside, and I've come into some silver…

I hear you're off to Calvary soon. I'm not sure where it is, but all the best.

Yours truly,

Judas

p.s. You drank out of that grail thing the last time we had supper together. Do you know where it went? Everyone is searching for it.

p.p.s. Do you still want me for a sunbeam?

ISLE OF WIGHT WRITERS DAY
Saturday 7th September 2024
9.15 a.m. – 5.00 p.m. at Carisbrooke Priory

- Are you a writer living on the Isle of Wight?
- Would you like to meet other people who love writing?
- Would you like to find out more about getting published?
- Do you have a published book (or books) that you would like to promote and sell?

If your answer to any of these questions is YES
then keep Saturday 7th September free for
Writers Day at Carisbrooke Priory

There will be opportunities for networking and conversation, plus
workshops, panel discussions, a bookstall, and much more.
Be sure to book early as places are limited.
(bring your own lunch – café open for tea and coffee)
Only £20 for the day plus £10 to promote
and sell your book on the bookstall.
More details to follow shortly.

Contact: Felicity Fair Thompson on ffair77@btinternet.com

Footprints On Slapton Sands by Felicity Fair Thompson

This year, Harry Beere would be ninety-two years old. He is the main character in my novel *The Kid on Slapton Beach*. It's late November 1943: the Admiralty's Notice to Leave by 20 December is distributed. Three thousand people are forced to leave the Devon coast at Christmas 1943, but why? Is an invasion coming?

Imagine packing up your life, not knowing where you will go or how you will cope. Businesses had to move. Farmers had to leave their land, remove all livestock, and dig up crops. Fishermen were forced away. Families had to pack up everything and leave the area without knowing why.

Wars have a great many secrets, and Exercise Tiger the D-Day rehearsal on Slapton Sands was one of the darkest. In 1943, the young US Servicemen flooded into Britain and, due to landing on D-Day beaches, were completely new to war. Rehearsing what going into combat was like was essential.

For Harry, who is twelve, leaving home is very worrying. His father is missing in action somewhere in Italy. His mother can't cope. His little sister is too young to understand. Helping a GI make friends with locals who are all very apprehensive about what is happening and where they will go, Harry makes a friend himself. He and GI Mike White get to know each other well in the lead-up to the exodus.

When Harry, his mother and little sister leave, his most precious possession, the one photograph of his father, is left behind. And Harry goes back for it – he's on that beach when Exercise Tiger happens.

Nearly thirty thousand men take part in secret full-scale rehearsals for the D-Day landings. Nearly a thousand men die. Everything, everything goes wrong! Harry's friend, GI Mike White, is on that beach. And Harry – Harry is, too…

His footprints were on that sand on the night of the ill-fated Exercise Tiger. My novel *The Kid on Slapton Beach* sells really well in Devon. My Harry would be ninety-two years old this year, and the Dartmouth Tourist Office asked me to make a film about Harry's memories and how he promised to keep the secret of Slapton Sands all his life.

The film will be shown in libraries, schools and community centres. The Apollo Theatre on the Island has been very helpful in providing actors and costumes, as has the Island's Video Club with old film and camera work, so there will be a special showing for them all

But we can all commemorate the fact it is 80 Years On this year since D-Day, the greatest amphibious landing the world has ever seen, and hear about the bravery and sacrifice of those ordinary people leaving home in Devon and the Allied troops involved there just five weeks earlier in such a difficult episode of WWII – the secret Exercise Tiger rehearsals on Slapton Sands. As President Harry Truman said: *The only thing new in the world is the history you don't know.*

Conservation by Hillard Morley

It was already over when he'd heard the shot.

He'd frozen. This was not a place for guns, he'd thought, but nonetheless, the sound had been alarming. Only a car backfiring, he'd decided and still a long way off, several floors below him in the street. There must be time to get away.

But he'd felt robbed and disadvantaged anyway. The silence and the peace of his activity had been shattered. Noise was against his nature, not enjoyable. He'd reached a peak so rarely scaled, and in pursuit of actions, he so rarely dared indulge that the lack of quiet to enjoy it had been galling. He'd not been allowed to savour the pleasure of the aftermath.

He'd had to dash away and leave her lying where she was. He'd run the risk of seeming cruel, he knew. He hadn't been indifferent, but briskly crossing the room, he'd washed her mess off his hands. He'd thought it was wise to leave immediately, although he'd cursed the waste, the insult to his future self. The worst was that in going quite so quickly, so lightly, he now couldn't fully remember. Of course, he'd hoped to be forgotten but had expected to be replete with memories – for what we can recall must need to endure.

He wishes that he'd stayed one moment more. He has a vague impression of her body, raw and open to him, sprawled out with her clothes still rumpled, though she'd made no movement to adjust them. She'd looked so vulnerable, he'd thought, and it'd crossed his mind she might just be asleep. But he'd made no attempt to rouse her as he'd made his hasty exit. Far too dangerous to stay; no point in waiting for the car outside to turn in at the gate, nor for the sound of slamming doors, a run of footsteps climbing up the stairs.

He'd headed for the balcony, swung over the rails and shimmied down the pipe the same way he'd got in. "Thanks," he'd had the courtesy to say. "I did enjoy that."

But she'd neither moved nor offered a reply.

And that, at least, was gratifying. No words were needed when a task was properly completed.

At the time, he'd been delighted that the ground below the window had been soft. It had muffled his landing, so awake or not, no one would have heard him from the house.

But now the thought of that same gentle earth, which had caught him kindly, cradled him so easily, begins to fill him with anxiety and dread

He's staring at the shoes he'd worn, so casually discarded, when he returned here last night. Only now does he see mud and tiny stones, the blades of grass packed into the tread.

He wonders what he has left behind. What evidence is being read at this moment? What says it of his habits and his character?

Footprints by Kate Young

We had recently moved to Bluebell Drive. The house was a bit rundown, but it was cheap. It was still more than we could afford, but we needed to move from our tiny one-bedroom flat because I was eight months pregnant with twins.

My husband, Josh, was in the front garden. Only two weeks earlier, it had been a complete jungle. Right now, Josh was laying concrete. The sun beat down on his blond hair, and I saw him straighten up to wipe away the sweat. A builder by trade, he knew what he was doing when it came to laying concrete.

Years ago, a television advert for Diet Coke featured a handsome man working outside – and being secretly admired by women indoors. "11.30, Diet Coke break!"

It is 11.30 am now, I noted, smiling to myself. I reached into the fridge for the jug of handmade lemonade, added ice cubes to two glasses, and took it all outside on a tray.

"That is why I love you, Rachel," Josh said.

He pulled up two patio chairs and an upended crate, then took the load from me.

"How's it going?" I asked.

"The new front path will be ready in no time."

We drank in companionable silence, listening to the drone of bees. Our neighbour had an impressive garden of flowers, lined with buddleia and lilac trees. Across the road two boys were playing football.

"Gosh, it's hot," I said. "I should have put my sunhat on."

"Relax, I'll get it!"

Josh was back moments later and was about to settle the hat on my head when I heard an ominous, whooshing sound.

"Look out!" I said as a football whizzed through the air and was heading for our windows.

Josh made a flying leap and grabbed it, leaving two footprints in the freshly laid concrete.

"Oops!" he said, good-naturedly.

He handed the ball back to the boys, who looked rather sheepish.

I felt a kick from inside me. "I hope the twins aren't going to be footballers!"

Josh laid a gentle hand on my stomach and felt the kicks. "I think they'll be champions.

I yawned. It was so hot. "I think I'd better go back inside."

Josh picked up the tray and followed me into the house. He put the half-empty jug back in the fridge. "Ooh – we're low on milk."

"I meant to get some, but forgot," I said.

"It must be baby brain," he laughed. "I'll go. You look like you need a rest."

I heard him drive away as I sank onto the sofa.

I was awoken by loud knocking. Feeling disorientated, I opened the front door to two police officers.

"Can we come in? There's been an accident…"

I stared past them at the two footprints hardening to grey as the dying light hit the new path.

Footprints by Graham Brown

In my seventh summer
the incoming tide
washed away any trace
of your footprints
as though you were never there.

I built a castle of sand
with turrets and paper flags,
searched rock pools for starfish,
scanned the horizon, foolishly
believing you would return.

On my journey home
I cradled a shell,
thought your voice was calling
above the ocean roar
until one day I heard no more.

Disguised as an old man,
I am back on that beach
still searching for mermaids and dragons.
The incoming tide
is closing in on my footprints.

Horizons Of Possibility by Word Spoken Song

Perched in a chair

third story window

holding in my hand

a fossilized fish jaw

that swam in this bay

as dinosaurs once grazed

her luxuriant marshlands

I look up then out
towards open infinite
horizons of possibilities

And in the far distance

a jet passenger aircraft

beneath a full glistening rainbow

rays of a setting sun

cruising into Gatwick radar locked

fifty miles distant

towering thunderclouds await

Will Gaia along

with the Great Mother Universe

that birthed her

purge their selves pristine

of this parasite

known to itself as Humanity

to catalyze the planet free?

Rainbows still shine above
the curve of Earth
Truth rocks Universe
sparks into Time

Infinite
horizons of possibilities
For Us To Choose

A Message from Word Spoken Song

We are kindred spirits drawn together here on the Island during 1990s by the smiling visage of The Buddha, whose eyes beam forth all are welcome, all is well. Our art is fuelled by an awareness of all those fellow seekers that have in the past seen/heard, are now seeing/hearing and in future times shall see/hear the beckoning doors of perception; the omnipresent sentient Universe always embracing touching our Earth. This is the Dreaming of our Storyline that inspires the music and lyrics. Delight your eyes and ears by scanning the QR code to see and hear our lyric video.

Thank you,
Mark & Matt

The Military Road by Chris Barnes

Where once they toiled
the scores and more of military men
to dig the road
to hack the chalk
to crush the rubble
load by load
carried from quarries
blown from the ground
dragged by cart
across fields and mounds
inch by inch
with adze and pick and mattock too

As they hacked at gorse
tore out tufted carpets of pinks
did they ever stop and stare
to gaze westward
eyes drawn down to the deep blue of the bay
then up, up to the High Down and beyond
west to Studland's distant shores

Will their footprints
still be there
their mark upon this land
fossilised amongst the stones and sand
or washed out to sea
in a milky white rim
like their road
slip, sliding away

The Return Visit by John Luckett

Earth Year 1951

The spaceship's last recorded visit was when the planet was a lush and verdant orb teeming with many life forms. It looked beautiful and appeared to be thriving, but the dominant species needed some help – badly.

Unaware of their precarious situation and heading for a self-inflicted mass extinction, they had already created the means and power to destroy the planet many times over. They would take all other life forms with them, which was not their right and the reason for the intervention.

The help was not immediately appreciated; it was greeted with outright hostility.

Similar planets to Earth existed throughout the Universe, but none as enigmatic. Its inhabitants were capable of limitless cruelty and depravity but could also demonstrate infinite love and compassion. The constant alternation between these two states of being left the planet constantly teetering on the brink of oblivion. Yet, there was something here, something unquantifiable that garnered hope.

Things could change here, couldn't they? Could they save themselves, or did they need guidance? On departure, they had been given a warning of the power of an outside intervention, if only a token one. What would be their response? The spaceship was here to find out.

Earth Year 2157

The spacecraft, resembling a shiny, revolving sphere, had landed on the planet's only satellite: a barren, desolate, lifeless landscape with a limited atmosphere called the Moon. The choice of landing site was deliberate and of historical significance. Ancient data revealed this place was once called *The Sea Of Tranquillity*. It also proved to be a suitable place for observations and measurements to establish the current state of the Earth.

Earth had lost its previous vivid, cobalt blue, white, and green appearance. The surface was invisible, and the atmosphere was a dull brown, puce-coloured mass of swirling gas clouds. Nothing could survive here; the planet was in its death throes, an irreversible process.

To one side, not far from the spacecraft, stuck in the lunar soil, was a metal pole with the final remains of some ragged material, which the nearby Sun's radiation had all but disintegrated. Around this pole were many footprints, the distinctive marks of the tread of primitive space boots. In Earth Year 1951, they were only dreaming of it, yet there was evidence that they actually made it here. This was where they took those first few steps.

It was time to leave. The spaceship gently rose. Vibrations from the craft's power source shook and shuffled the loose lunar surface below. The metal pole fell, and the footprints were erased to become like the rest of the anonymous terrain surrounding them as if they had never existed.

There would be no need for a return visit.

Leaving Footprints At Alum Bay by Emily Gillatt-Ball

"Alum" was a word we didn't know, but never asked what it meant. When both your parents are teachers, you learn quickly not to ask questions like that. The holiday mood would have been crushed underfoot like a butterfly, as Dad spotted another educational opportunity.

Other parents might have answered:

"It's some sort of mineral – I expect they used to mine it there."

or

"I don't know, dear. Would you like a cheese sandwich?"

Dad, on the other hand, would have spent twenty minutes explaining from memory exactly what alum was, its uses in the dyeing and tanning industries and how, despite the name, alum was *not* mined there and hadn't even been found there.

But once the question had been answered more fully than the most enthusiastic questioner could ever want, there was no stopping the tide: he would move on to the complete history of Alum Bay, how Marconi did radio experiments there in Victorian times and, as an exciting bonus topic, exactly why the word 'aluminium' was spelled and pronounced differently in America.

Meanwhile, we would be shuffling our plimsolls on the gravel car park, longing to get to the beach, and glaring at the foolish sister who had asked the question.

The one thing we knew already about Alum Bay was its fame for having many different colours of natural sand. Near the top of the cliff was a wooden-fronted shop, where you could buy a glass lighthouse, bell or Isle of Wight shape to fill with stripes of the coloured sand. You could either use the trays of sand in the shop or carry the chosen container down to the beach and collect your own sands. We chose the latter option, then set off, eagerly clutching the cheapest lighthouses, down the cliff on a seemingly endless series of steps.

Contrary to my expectations, the beach was not made of rainbow stripes of coloured sand. In fact, apart from a strip of sand at the water's edge, it was covered with chunky pebbles, awkward to walk upon with our small feet. The sands had to be scraped from the soft rocks of the cliff, as we clambered about excitedly, looking for new colours and comparing our stripes. Once filled, the glass tubes were propped up on a crumpled anorak while we paddled briefly in the chilly sea and made patterns of footprints on the wet sand. We all sat on rocks and munched ham rolls, taking turns with Dad's heavy binoculars to look at the distant lighthouse and the boat giving rides around the Needles.

Finally, we toiled laboriously to the summit, holding our lighthouses carefully to avoid spilling their precious sands. At last, we reached the wooden shop, where the man added extra sand and deftly tamped in a cork to hold the stripes in place. As we settled back in the car and admired our finished lighthouses, we all agreed that Alum Bay was a great place, whatever "alum" might mean.

The Ice Hotel by David Goodday

Snow pillows support my weary head,
and ice sheets cover my frozen bed.
Just an ice block away is our local store,
but I'm finding it hard to step out of the door.

There's no central heating, and no flushing loos,
just white frosted windows with cold arctic views.
The footprints outside won't last very long,
one minute there, the next minute gone.

There's nothing built here that's designed to stay,
that's why this hotel will soon melt away.
But when that day comes and new hopes arise,
I will be sitting under sunnier skies.

Ventnor by Chris Rickards

Halfway up the Downs
I turn to gaze…on Ventnor
that perfect of imperfect towns
enfolded in the arms of the bay.

How I love that crazy place –
perhaps my soul's rest on earth.
Populated by life's eccentrics:
men in shorts year-round,
golden-skinned sunbathers,
a handful of kilt-wearers
migrated from the colder Scottish climes
and Ventnorians – proud of the name.

The ebb and flow of the tide
pulsates through Ventnor's life.

As the tide turns, so does the weather.

Guarded by the Downs
yet endangered by the blue clay
bit by bit
Ventnor
slips
into
the
sea…

Footprints On A Walk by Maggie Brown

People you miss and who love you leave footprints in your heart forever. Physical footprints cannot last long, whether in the snow, mud or sand. On this rainy February day, I'm bound to see footprints when I venture out. There's a break in the clouds, so I walk a little over a mile from home to the beach at Freshwater Bay. I pass through a gate into a field known locally as "Granny's Mead" and follow the path. A plaque informs me that it is named after Elizabeth Stephens ("Granny"), a community midwife who worked in Freshwater for fifty years. A large oak tree with dark, skeletal branches stands in the field.

I reach the end and turn left onto a road. On the green bank opposite, the first snowdrops are opening their tiny, delicate flowers. A few yellow primroses are also in bloom: a hope for spring. At the road's intersection is a grocer's shop with a notice that states it's stood there since 1865. Today, footprints are left in the mud outside; one never knows who left their imprint here.

Just a few yards away, down the road, stands a small church dedicated to St Agnes. Its thatched roof and wooden bell turret make it a unique sight, a testament to the rich history of this place. As I step inside, dust on the church floor reveals the footprints of those who have come before me, a silent reminder of the lives that have passed through here.

Keeping on the right-hand side of the road, I pass Dimbola House, a museum and gallery dedicated to Julia Margaret Cameron, a pioneer photographer who bought the property and lived here from 1860 to 1875.

Nearby are numerous footprints leading from a gate onto Tennyson Down. The sea is within sight.

As I continue along the path, the beauty of nature unfolds before me. A hedge has small hawthorn trees growing in its midst. The melodious song of a robin stops me in my tracks. To my pleasure, I see it perched on a branch. And then, a few metres away, stretches Freshwater Bay.

The grey sea has huge wind-whipped waves following a gale and rain. It is a raging force, with waves crashing onto the promenade and bringing numerous stones. In the sand, I notice human footprints and dog pawprints swiftly swept away.

How different in the summer, when gentle waves lap the shore, and people enjoy the beach. In my reverie, I fail to notice the giant wave heading my way, the spray enveloping me. Saltwater smothers my face, leaving its taste on my tongue.

I retrace my steps, leaving my footprints in the sand. Soon, they too will disappear.

Footprints by Steve Taverner

On the southwest coast of the Isle of Wight, in an area rich in dinosaur fossils, is a wave-cut platform containing what are believed to be the footprints of the dinosaur Iguanadon. A friend of mine, Helen, twisted her ankle while walking over this ledge. I liked the idea that she may have trodden on one of these footprints and that one animal's actions could directly affect another a hundred million years later. [S.T.]

When dinosaurs walked on the land,
                    they left deep footprints in the sand.
As buried sand was pressurized, the footprints became fossilized.
A hundred million years went past, when Helen tried to walk too fast
upon the rocks with footprints deep, with flimsy shoes upon her feet.
Her foot went over. "Ouch," she cried.
                              "I must have stepped upon the side
of a deep dent a dino made. This broken foot's the price I've paid."
I wonder if Iguanadon when making footprints way back yon,
assessed the risk of damage to poor Helen's foot that he might do.
It's harsh to give him too much blame, for what we do is just the same.
The footprints that we leave behind are huge, yet we give little mind
to other species living now, let alone considering how
we might affect what's yet to come, and we think dinosaurs were dumb!

Remains by Tony Hands

The receding waters
leave signs of low tide life
in rock pools:
crabs and shrimps, seaweed,
weird seeming plants.

Along the cretaceous coast,
among sand-exposed rocks
are fossilised trees, and footprints
of creatures long extinct.
(I think of the iguanodon.)

While the remains of
today's beach visitors
are swallowed by water,
reclaimed by sand,
leaving no trace.

Two Sets by Jenny Tudor

The beach is empty, not a soul in sight,
no one to hear me, to hear of my plight.
I walk to the sea, the seagulls with me
their cries echo mine, my struggle with the brine.

I'll swim and swim 'til I'm quite worn out.
I'll sink to the depths, with never a doubt.

But suddenly, I hear your gentle voice:
"Head for the shore, my love, and rejoice.
Just listen to me and stay in the zone.
I promised I'd never leave you alone."

As I wandered back, my heart full of sighs,
two sets of footprints now greeted my eyes.
How could I ever have doubted your word,
I cried out for help, and as ever you heard.

Two sets of footprints, we'll stroll together,
across golden sands, forever and ever.

Once Upon A Land by Callanan Harris

Once upon a land in a time long ago
vegetables, fruit and flowers did grow

Once upon a land in a time long ago
summer was sun and winter was snow

Once upon a land in a time long ago
oceans were deep and rivers did flow

Once upon a land in a time long ago
all species roamed freely to and fro

Once upon a land in a time long ago
POTUS pressed the red button
all his generals screamed NO!!!

We watched in stunned silence
from our base on Mars
as our world imploded among the stars…

Erin's Ed by Maureen Shaw O'Neill

This delicate piece by Maureen Shaw O'Neill is a fond farewell to an IOW legend of the folk scene, Ed Jeffares, who has left his footprints in the hearts of his folk friends. He would always turn up with a tripod and camera to record singers and dancers at the many venues on the Island. He had a smile for everyone, and captured many a folk music moment, though he struggled with diabetes and painful feet.

The end of the road for Ed,
his soul passed through Ireland's bed.
So quietly he left us,
his legacy – his precious photos.

There is more: his videos,
stilled now just for a while.
The time will come for a smile
when we will replay them,
mile after mile.

Thank you, chap of the *Curragh*,
from tank to tunes to *Rince*
to *Sasana* you sailed.

To this very Island of Wight
you captured it just right.
Slan Anocht
Go safely; goodbye tonight.

Translations from the Gaelic
Rince = dancing
Sasana = England
Slan Anocht = Goodbye Tonight

Badger Footprints by Jamie Britton

About The Contributors

Chris Barnes is a retired teacher, lecturer and garden designer. Her collection of personal, travel and nature journals have inspired a blog on her website, and now her short stories and poetry. Born on the Isle of Wight, she still lives at her beloved Freshwater Bay.

Olha Bereza has a degree in Psychology. She is fluent in Russian, Ukrainian, and English, is Editor-in-Chief of *The NorthStar Online Journal* and author of *Four Seasons of the Green Land* as Holley Dovetail. She lives on IOW and focuses on children's education. As a member of the London Group of Multilingual Writers, she organises weekly online Creative Writing classes for teenagers.

Anmarie Bowler (see page 27).

Annys Brady is native to the IOW, has two children and works as a teacher. In 2021 she was longlisted for the National Poetry Competition which, she comments, was "a lovely surprise". Annys enjoys writing but doesn't have as much time to devote to it as she would like.

Jamie Britton has taught English, English Literature and Film for over forty years (twenty on IOW). Having a lifelong interested in cartoons, he has published in national and regional papers and magazines. His favourite cartoonists are Leo Baxendale and Don Martin. Being rather a Luddite, Jamieson draws only in pen and ink.

Graham Brown has written and performed poetry for many years. He runs regular Open Mic poetry events in Newport, Ryde and East Cowes and also has a creative writing group at East Cowes Library. His latest collection of poems *Rainbows In The Dark* was published by Naked Figleaf Press.

Maggie Brown started writing stories at a young age after winning a Cadbury's National Essay Competition. Her prize was lots of chocolate. She has written stories for her grandchildren and joined creative writing groups in the many places she has lived. She has had several stories and poems published.

Yvonne Brown was born in Dunoon, Scotland. She moved to the Island in 2003 having written poetry for several years. She has performed her poetry in Newcastle, Edinburgh and at the Hastings International Poetry Festival. She is still writing, although her appearances have been restricted by poor health in recent years.

Andrew Butcher is a writer & performer currently dabbling in self-reflective rumination after donning masks for many years. Following a theatrical solo show debut 'Fake It Till You break It!' at Ventnor Fringe '23, he has created a companion show 'I Knew You', an 'eras tour' of poetry about the identity of our art and how it changes as we do.

Marion Carmichael has a life-long love of words. She has published poems in small magazines and *The Shore Women*, a collection of poems by Island writers. Her own collection *Grass Green Stockings* was winner of the Isle of Wight fiction award for 2022. She is currently writing a book based on her grandmother's life.

Meryl Clark started to write "the novel" sixteen years ago, but life – in the shape of grandchildren – got in the way. Now she spends 95% of her time on IOW, Meryl has picked up the threads, joined The Write Place writing group, and hopes to finish it! She enjoys writing poetry and short stories, so the dratted novel is still on the back burner. But who knows….

Tim Cooper is MAWGIAS – a middle-aged white guy in a suit – when he's performing at slams across the country. But here on the page he's just Tim Cooper, an Island lad earning a living wherever and however he can. Tim won the Dublin Story Slam in October 2019.

J. W. Edge has written stories and poems from the age of nine. It was not until work ceased and her family were grown that the stories started to be written in earnest. With encouragement from a local writers group, three novels, many short stories, and poems are progressing towards publication.

Darren Everest is better known for his skills in horticulture than literature, especially his expertise in dahlias and sweet peas. He write the occasional article for the *National Dahlia Society* and has a monthly column in *IW Observer*. In May 2024 he won gold medal for his sweet peas at the prestigious Royal Chelsea Flower Show.

Eric Ferris hales from Portchester and has lived on IOW for thirty-four years. His working life has varied considerably, from musician to scientist. He has published poems in small press books and pamphlets. He loves writing about myth, fable, folklore, nature and the gods, and is always looking to find some magic below the seemingly mundane surface.

Norman Figueiredo has lived on the Island for eight years. He worked in clerical work in the private/public sector. His love of poetry began in his early teens years. He enjoys "exploring the margins of words and expressions". He was part of a poetry group on the Island and has produced five booklets of poetry.

Ross Glanfield is a musician, songwriter and occasional poet. He performs at Figgy Gigs, and around IOW. He is preparing to record his debut single in 2024.

Jean G-Owen founded Naked Figleaf Press and Naked Figleaf Collective. She has published poetry, essays, edited volumes, short stories and reviews. She performs with The Triple Crones. *Bites of Love: Poems & Images* was published in 2023. She is working on her novel *The Poacher's Daughter*, which is forthcoming in 2024.

Emily Gillatt-Ball lives in a Victorian cottage in Ryde, where she runs creative writing groups and writes family history, memoirs, poetry and short stories. Her first novel is currently being revised, and she is now working on a historical romance set on the Isle of Wight.
emilygillattball.co.uk.

David Goodday has won many prizes, including Writers Bureau Student Competition 2019, third prize at Sight for Wight Short Story 2022, and runner-up in Sight For Wight 2019. His first children's book, *The Search For Donkey Paradise*, is due out in 2024. David is a member of East Cowes Creative Writing group, and hopes readers enjoy his stories and poems as much as he enjoys writing them.

Tina Goode has enjoyed drawing and painting since childhood. She returned to creating art when asked to help run a community art group and was encouraged in her work by the art tutor. Since then she has developed distinctive styles in lino cutting, book making, and pen and ink art. She was delighted to be asked to help illustrate Becky Haydock's poem.
Follow her on Facebook: Inkstone Arts

Tony Hands was born in Coventry, made his way slowly south. He loves the spoken word, aims for eclectic out-of-the-box writing, some humorous, others poignant. Tony is into nature, paddle boarding, reading and learning new things. He hates liars and bullies, and currently enjoys his work trying to make a positive difference to homeless people.

Callanan Harris (Jeanette Harris) is an Irish writer of verse and short stories living on the Isle of Wight. Her first book of verse *Shite & Shinola* was published in 2022.

Becky Haydock got sick with multiple sclerosis two years ago and had to give up work. To fill the days, she started writing and has since produced two novels and some poetry. She has learned many things through writing, especially that her mind remains creative and lively. She has proven to herself that even living with MS, you can be a capable, and active member of the Island's writing community.

Cat James is a newspaper columnist who writes thought-provoking discourses, ranging from celebrating invertebrates to bingo, public realm alternatives to dog costumes. She is passionate about sustainability, women's issues, creeping digitalisation, climate emergency, among other topics and incorporating humorous anidon. She performs her essays at spoken word events.

Sandy Kealty comes from a talented family. Her grandfather was a storyteller, her grandmother a music hall singer who wore a large hat. Sandy's inevitable path was to become a poet and performer, dancing to the music of language whilst casting a keen eye over the ups and downs of life. An Island resident for twenty years, she currently lives on the Welsh Borders. "I always preferred the edges of things," she comments.

https://skealty.wixsite.com/skealty

Diana Kimpton lives in Cowes and has written over forty books for children. She has written articles and books for adults, and several scripts for screen and stage. She particularly enjoys writing about animals and making people laugh – often at the same time.

https://www.dianakimpton.co.uk

Ricky Lock has been writing for over twenty years. Many of his short stories and poems have been published in books and magazines in UK and America. He is also an artist, painting in many media, and working on commissions. He has exhibited across the Island, including The Open Studio. He sells his painted art cards at local outlets.

John Luckett works full-time at Mountbatten Hospice. He attends local writing groups and describes himself as "an aspiring writer". Recently, John completed Level 3 Diploma in Creative Writing through distance learning and is working on a thriller novel. He has a second writing project, collaborating with a local artist.

Cheryl May (see page 19).

Peter May was buoyed at having ten comedy sketches published by *Lazy Bee*, and so joined The Write Place writing group in Freshwater. He was delighted to have his short stories included in the group's anthology. He adds: "I submit them with a beguiling modesty as I have much to be modest about."

Hillard Morley (see pages 38-41).

Pat Murgatroyd is a member of The Poetry Society and the Isle of Wight Stanza and has been widely published in national magazines. She belongs to writing groups on the Isle of Wight, Romsey and Winchester. She greatly enjoys performing and has read her work at Ventnor Fringe, Medina Bookshop, and Arundel and Winchester Literary Festivals among others. Poems are always running in her head.

https://poems.poetrysociety.org.uk/poets/pat-murgatroyd/

Chris Rickards is a retired Drama and Theatre Studies Lecturer/Teacher who now fulfils a long-held desire to write poetry. She is on the WI Speakers' list, sings, enjoys country dancing and recently edited *Etrurian Poppies*, a collection of nature poems by Sister Patricia Bolton.

Eleanor Roddick worked in the NHS as commissioner, developing the Island's urgent care and cancer services. She has an eclectic Celtic and Anglo-Saxon heritage and is drawn to prehistoric-era fiction based on research, pagan belief systems, and personal connection. She has many stories to tell.

Steve Rushton (see page 5).

Maggie Sawkins moved from Portsmouth to Brading in 2021. Her collections include *The Zig Zag Woman, Zones of Avoidance*, and *The House Where Courage Lives*. She holds an MA with distinction in Creative Writing and is the recipient of a Ted Hughes Award for New Work in Poetry.
    https://iwcreativenetwork.com/directory/magpieisle/profile/

Lisa Scovell-Strickland was born and raised on the Island. When not steeping gin, making jam, or writing poetry, she can be found enjoying the delights of the countryside with her wife and two Norse gods, Thor and Loki. Her debut collection *The Shaping of Me* was published in July 2023. Her second collection is forthcoming in 2024.

Maureen Shaw O'Neill hasn't published yet but keeps threatening to gather her writings together one day! She has performed with Steve Love in 'Ireland to the Island' at Monkton Arts. She also performs at The Priory Poetry Group, The Waverley, and Chillerton clubs, as well as on the mainland clubs when visiting them.

Steve Taverner (see page 63).

Felicity Fair Thompson was the first woman on Rank's West End Cinema management. Her film *Carisbrooke Castle* was broadcast on SKY, and other films aired on Australian television. Felicity is a prolific writer of children's books, magazine features, theatre reviews, plays, poetry, novels. She won three awards at Screenplay Festivals in 2023.
    https://www.felicityfairthompson.co.uk

Jenny Tudor belongs to The Write Place writing group at Freshwater Library and enjoys recounting her memoirs. More recently she has developed her poetry writing skills. Jenny looks forward to submitting poems to *The Figlet*.

Julie Watson has written two collections of travel stories, mostly recently *Travel Takeaways: Around the World in Forty Tales* (Beachy Books, 2023). She is currently working on a humorous book about the challenges of living with a single-minded rescue cat. She is retired, lives in Cowes, kayaks on the western Yar, and indulges in travelling.

https://beachybooks.com/bookshop/julie-watson

Heather Whatley lives in Yarmouth and enjoys the many creative opportunities available on the Island. She writes her own material for her comedy sketches, which she performs at monthly Figgy Gigs. She also plays saxophone in a duo with her husband on guitar.

Karl Whitmore is an adult human of average height and wears size 10 shoes (coincidentally the same size as his Wacom tablet.) He loves being part of Naked Figleaf Press and working with other people to help bring stories and poetry to life. He currently likes the word 'cromulent'.

Ian Winter grew up in Ryde and is an "occasional poet". When he was able to drive, he found the Military Road and thought how nice it would be to live around there. He's lived in a restored farm building for the past twenty-five years: family, sun, mud, dog, rain, the lot.

Word Spoken Song (see page 94).

Kate Young was highly commended in the Hastings International Poetry Competition 2002 and won the Isle of Wight Literary Festival 2012 flash fiction competition. Her novella featured in The Paul Cave Prize for Literature 2023 anthology. She has just been long-listed in a national flash fiction competition, and leads MAD Scribblers Writers' and Illustrators' Café, East Cowes.

The Figlet Issue Three Winter 2025

Deadline for Submission:
30 September 2024

Featured Theme:

FIGHT OR FLIGHT

Terms & Conditions

1. Submit poems on any topic (no more than three poems, no longer than **30 lines**).

OR

2. One fiction or non-fiction piece on any topic (no more than **750 words**).

3. Authors are invited to enter one poem (no more than **30 lines**) or one fiction or non-fiction piece (no more than **750 words**) in addition to the general submissions to the featured theme.

4. Each piece of writing to be typed on a separate sheet of **A4** paper in **Times New Roman, 12 point**. Please DO NOT include fancy fonts or symbols.

5. Submissions which DO NOT meet THE FIGLET'S specifications will be disregarded.

6. Submissions to be the author's own original work.

7. All copyright remains with the individual author.

8. Anonymous submissions will NOT be considered.

9. Final decision rests with the Editor. No correspondence about such decisions will be entered into with individual authors.

10. Submissions to arrive no later than the deadline:
30 September 2024

About Naked Figleaf Press

Naked Figleaf Press is a small independent press founded in Summer 2023 by Jean G-Owen. At Naked Figleaf Press, we give a fig about publishing writers we live on the Isle of Wight. We publish poetry, novellas, essays and other types of non-fiction, short story collections and memoirs.

Publications so far include:

Bites of Love: Poems and Images by Jean G-Owen
Rainbows in the Dark by Graham Brown
Scar on the Rock by Steve Taverner
Not Just Desserts by Cheryl May
The Figlet Literary Magazine Issue One Winter Season 2024

Coming Soon:
The Triple Crones by Jean G-Owen, Sandy Kealty & Cheryl May

We publish a bi-annual literary magazine titled *The Figlet*

We invite submissions from IOW writers
No unsolicited material will be considered

Enquiries to be sent via email to Jean G-Owen:

jean28owen@gmail.com

Naked Figleaf Press

We Give A Fig